AMERICAN HERITAGE
ILLUSTRATED HISTORY
OF THE UNITED STATES

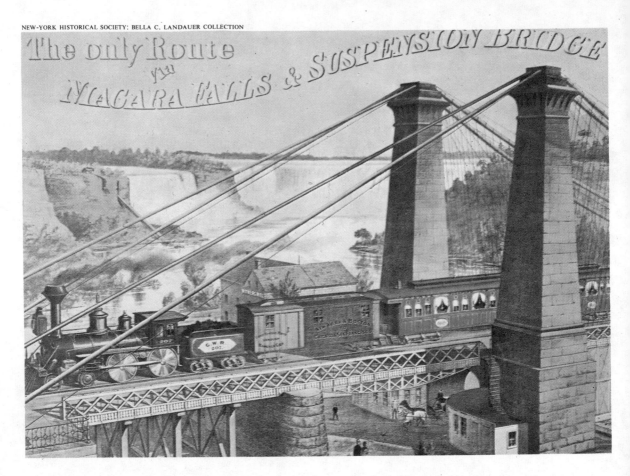

A poster for the New York & Boston Railroad reminds the public that only one route gives them a view of the great Niagara Falls on their trip west.

FRONT COVER: *The Wason railroad car manufacturers of Springfield, Massachusetts, in an 1872 advertising poster.*
NEW YORK HISTORICAL SOCIETY: BELLA C. LANDAUER COLLECTION

FRONT ENDSHEET: *On the Occasion of the World's Fair in Philadelphia in 1876, a "centennial mirror" reflected 100 years of progress in the United States.*
LIBRARY OF CONGRESS

CONTENTS PAGE: *The Brotherhood of Locomotive Engineers, founded in April, 1863, as the first railroad union, gave this certificate to each member.*
NEW YORK HISTORICAL SOCIETY; BELLA C. LANDAUER COLLECTION

BACK ENDSHEET: *An 1865 painting of the Bethlehem, Pennsylvania, steel plant shows a Bessemer converter (background) and workers pouring molten steel.*
BETHLEHEM STEEL COMPANY

BACK COVER: *As the railroads continued to expand to the west (top), they encountered many hazards: prairie fires, unfriendly Indians, and stubborn herds of buffalo, as in this painting; Thomas Edison (below left) worked 72 straight hours on his phonograph; detail of a poster (below right) announcing the Union Pacific's opening of transcontinental rail route.*
SMITHSONIAN INSTITUTION; EDISON NATIONAL HISTORICAL SITE; UNION PACIFIC RAILROAD

AMERICAN HERITAGE ILLUSTRATED HISTORY OF THE UNITED STATES

VOLUME 10

AGE OF STEEL

BY ROBERT G. ATHEARN

Created in Association with the
Editors of AMERICAN HERITAGE

and for the updated edition
MEDIA PROJECTS INCORPORATED

CHOICE PUBLISHING, INC.

New York

Library of Congress Catalog Card Number: 87-73399
ISBN 0-945260-12-1
ISBN 0-945260-00-8

This 1988 edition is published and distributed by Choice Publishing, Inc., 53 Watermill Lane, Great Neck, NY 11021 by arrangement with American Heritage, a division of Forbes, Inc.

Manufactured in the United States of America
10 9 8 7 6 5 4 3

CONTENTS OF THE COMPLETE SERIES

Editor's Note to the Revised Edition
Introduction by ALLAN NEVINS
Main text by ROBERT G. ATHEARN

EACH VOLUME CONTAINS AN ENCYCLOPEDIC SECTION; MASTER INDEX IN VOLUME 18

CONTENTS OF VOLUME 10

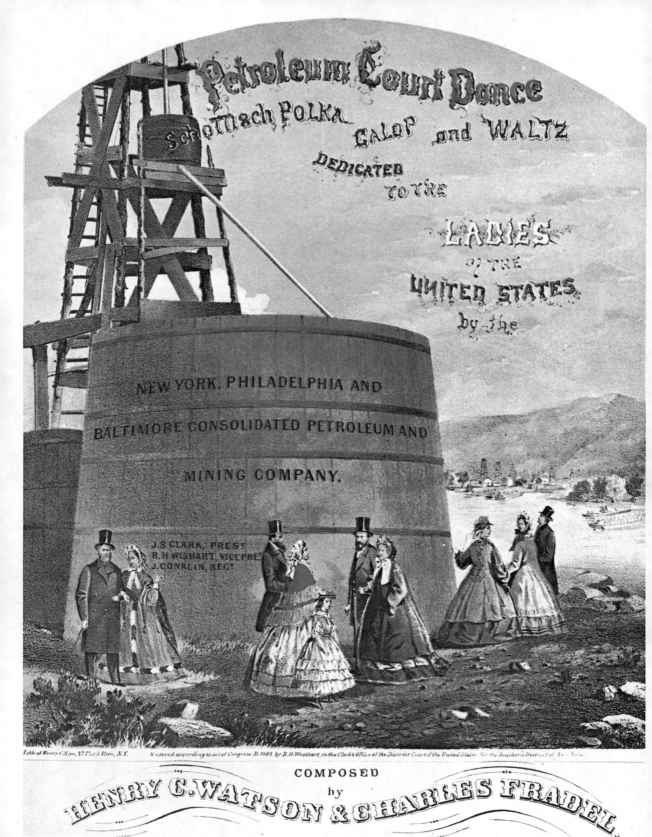

814

CHAPTER 28

INDUSTRIAL AMERICA

The guns of the Civil War were stilled, the banners were furled, and the survivors made their way homeward. The Confederate veteran found a ruined land. To Carl Schurz, a former Union general touring the South for President Andrew Johnson, the countryside "looked for many miles like a broad black streak of ruin and desolation." By contrast, the North had shot ahead. "Everywhere wartime industrialization had brought signs of growth," John Hope Franklin wrote. "What Union soldier could not quicken his pace as he moved not only nearer his loved ones but also closer to what would surely be a glorious future!"

For if the war had left many a sleeve empty and many a home bereaved, it had also left the nation a precious legacy—the North's magnificent industrial machine. The time for running it at full speed had never been better. From its beginnings a decade before, the Republican Party had adopted the businessman. For half a

In 1865, six years after the first well was drilled, an oil firm dedicated these dances to the ladies of the United States.

century after the war, it would continue to nurture him with favorable tariff, banking, railroad, and immigration legislation, and with all manner of general favors. Underlying this auspicious political climate was nature's bounteous inheritance. Copper, iron, oil, coal, gold, silver, timber, and almost limitless free land awaited exploitation. Virtually untouched before mid-century, the American West was a rich empire filled with treasures. Add to all this the human component —a bold group of entrepreneurs to mine the treasures, inventors and scientists to provide them with tools— and there emerged a combination bound to produce an economic revolution.

Andrew Carnegie, John D. Rockefeller, James J. Hill, William K. Vanderbilt—yes, even Jim Fisk and John W. "Bet You a Million" Gates —merely to repeat the names is to call up one of the gaudiest eras in American history.

The rich empire that awaited exploitation was not easy to subdue. It was a vast land of high mountains, rushing rivers, and climates that could be devastatingly cruel. Often the treasures were buried deep in the ground or located in places well-nigh inaccessible from established centers of population and production. A wrong guess—or a forest fire or a severe snowstorm—could make the difference between wealth and ruin. And in the absence of the type of regulatory legislation that we know today, the development of these resources was a dog-eat-dog business. "Indeed, under present-day rules," Stewart H. Holbrook has written, "[many of these industrialists] would face a good hundred years in prison. . . . These were tough-minded fellows, who fought their way encased in rhinoceros hides and filled the air with their mad bellowings and the cries of the wounded. . . ." Yet together they built an era that as much as any other has made America great.

The steel industry and its master, Andrew Carnegie, thoroughly exemplify the age and its spirit. The Kelley-Bessemer process, a cheap method of reducing molten pig iron into refined steel, was perfected during the 1850s, when Carnegie, a poor Scottish immigrant's son, was finding his feet in the New World as a bobbin boy and messenger in Pennsylvania. Simultaneously, huge deposits of iron ore were discovered in the great Mesabi Range of northern Minnesota.

Carnegie entered the steel industry shortly after the Civil War, and within 15 years reached the top. In 1882, he pooled his interests with Henry Clay Frick, who dominated the coke industry in Pittsburgh, and together they gained control of all the Mesabi Range ore they needed. From that point on, their only problem was competition, which they handled with ruthless aplomb.

A story with different characters but the same plot can be told of the oil industry. When "Colonel" E. L. Drake struck oil at Titusville, Pennsylvania, in 1859, the rush for "black gold" was on. Hundreds of prospectors sank wells, but a shrewd young commission merchant named John Davison Rockefeller was to make the most money. In 1860, he invested his savings of $700; in two years his stake became $4,000. In 1870, Rockefeller and some associates formed the Standard Oil Company of Ohio, capitalized at $1,000,000.

Standard Oil is a prime example of industrial success in the growing nation. After 1870, clear of debt and obligated to no one, it began to buy up smaller producers or force them to the wall. Growth meant power. The company now connected its expanding units with pipelines, thus not only increasing efficiency but forcing the railroads to submit to Standard Oil's demands. Soon the railroads were conspiring with Standard, to the ruin of other petroleum producers. Because it got secret rebates, or "kickbacks," on tank-car shipments, Rockefeller's company could deal fatal blows to its competitors.

By 1881, the policy of independence and maintenance of cash reserves pro-

In an 1866 photograph, Edwin L. Drake (wearing a top hat) stands near the world's first oil well, which he drilled in 1859 at Titusville, Pennsylvania.

duced a working backlog of $45,000,-000. The Standard Oil Trust was established and began to draw banks and railroads into its web. By 1895, its cash assets amounted to $150,000,000.

Alongside the names of Carnegie and Rockefeller stood those of other big-business captains. Hormel, Armour, Swift, and Cudahy came to dominate the meat-packing industry.

817

In finance, which made everything else possible, the name of John Pierpont Morgan led all the rest.

Tinkerers and inventors

Until relatively recent times, the United States has produced few men who may be called pure scientists. Of the 18 men whose likenesses were originally chosen to adorn the Washington headquarters of our National Academy of Sciences, only two were Americans—Josiah Willard Gibbs, who was professor of mathematical physics at Yale for 30 years, and Benjamin Franklin. The leisure and intellectual atmosphere in which original contributions to theoretical physics, chemistry, or biology are most often produced were absent in the hustling, bustling, still-to-be-built America of the 18th and 19th centuries. Its people were too busy laying railroad track, mining gold, sinking oil wells, and building steel mills to give much thought to theories.

But tinkering, inventing, and figuring out how things work and how to make them work better—that is something else again. With men of this turn of mind the Republic has been richly blessed. The young immigrant Samuel Slater, memorizing the plans for an entire English cotton-spinning mill and reproducing it in alien Rhode Island; Robert Fulton working to perfect his steamboat; Eli Whitney visiting a Southern cotton plantation and figuring out how to separate the seeds from the fiber; Samuel Colt devising a revolver with interchangeable parts—all these men and their achievements are familiar stories of the pre-Civil War era.

The war greatly stimulated that inventive spirit, and the industrial expansion that followed brought it to full flower. Americans got a chance to see two of the most important men of the period—although they paid them little attention at first—at the Philadelphia Centennial Exposition of 1876. In a small booth in the Machinery Hall, a young Scot named Alexander Graham Bell was exhibiting a newfangled gadget he called a telephone. "My God!" exclaimed the visiting emperor of Brazil when he heard Bell's voice over the wire. "It talks." The other important exhibitor was Thomas Alva Edison, a 29-year-old "tramp" telegrapher who had already improved the stock ticker and the telegraph and invented wax wrapping paper and the mimeograph machine.

If any one man symbolizes the American spirit of invention, surely it is Edison, "The Wizard of Menlo Park." On an estate in that New Jersey town, he set up during the centennial year a shop whose motto was "Inventions To Order." Throughout the next half-century, there were to pour forth from his fertile imagination a dozen devices that would profoundly alter the lives of all who came after him—the first commercially practical incandescent light bulb, the electric generator, the phonograph, important contributions to the movie

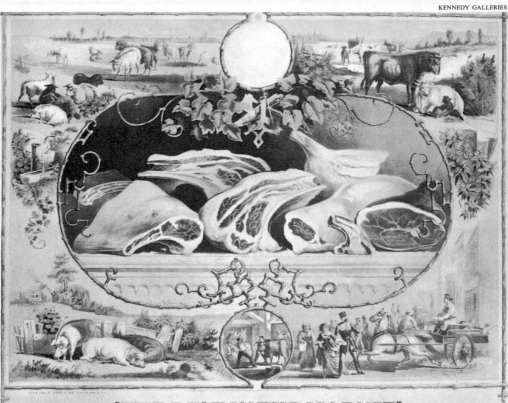

"THE BEST IN THE MARKET."

Chicago's Union Stockyards in 1866 (below) used to ship livestock to local dealers until Gustavus Swift in 1875 began slaughtering animals in the yards and shipping the meat, as advertised in a meat packer's poster above.

NEW-YORK HISTORICAL SOCIETY

Steel mills along the Monongahela, one of the three rivers flowing through Pittsburgh, were painted by the primitive Pennsylvania artist John Kane.

industry. In his lifetime, he was granted 1,093 patents, more than any other man in American history. Progress, he had reason to know, is as much the product of persistence as of pure genius: To develop a durable filament for his incandescent bulb, he tried coconut fibers, lampwick, and hairs taken from a friend's beard before finally hitting upon a thread of carbonized paper. "There's a better way to do it," he repeatedly told the young men who worked for him. "Find it!"

In those years between Lincoln and McKinley, other persistent, inventive young men were tinkering with gadgets that were to make the achievements of the masters of industry possible. Carnegie himself backed T. T. Woodruff, who created a railroad sleeping car. After they pooled their resources with George M. Pullman, long-distance passenger travel by rail became bearable. In 1869, George Westinghouse received a patent on a railroad air brake. Previously, the brakes of each car of a train had to be operated separately; with the air brake, an engineer sitting in his cab could slow a long string of freight or passenger cars to a smooth stop. Westinghouse's brake, along with his electrical signal-control system, made the high-speed trains of Hill and Vanderbilt manageable and safe.

Later, with the help of Hungarian-born Nikola Tesla and in competition with Edison, Westinghouse would develop a practical means of supplying electric current to homes, cities, and industries. This revolutionary source of light and power was to become so essential to modern society that in 1931, when Edison died and someone proposed that all of America's electric lights and power be turned off for a moment or two in his honor, President Hoover was obliged to reject the idea. The result would have been chaos.

Arteries of steel

Enterprising leadership, inventive genius, rich resources, and a sympathetic government helped bring the industrial era to birth, but without one more factor it would never have got beyond the nursery. This was the iron horse.

So important was the spread of rail transportation that the decades after the Civil War have often been called the railroad era. Service east of the Mississippi was expanded and im-proved, but the most dramatic growth took place in the West. From 35,000 miles of road in operation in 1865, the network of tracks across the country grew to 258,000 miles before 1900.

The so-called transcontinentals attracted much attention—especially the first one, built jointly by the Union Pacific and the Central Pacific. After 1869, when the Union Pacific and the Central Pacific met at Promontory Summit in Utah, lines streaked westward. By 1870, the Kansas Pacific reached Denver. During the next 20 years, the Southern Pacific, the Atchison, Topeka & Santa Fe, the Northern Pacific, and the Great Northern all made West Coast connections.

The growth of the early railroad industry was, in a peculiarly American way, a romance. But that growth was American in another sense, too: It was marked by great speed and waste. In 1862, to encourage construction across the Great American Desert, the federal government offered every other section of a 10-mile-square tract of land for every mile of road built. Two years later, when this proved not attractive enough, the offer was doubled. Eventually, railroads received from state and federal governments a total of 155,504,994 acres—an area almost the size of Texas. In addition, extensive loans were made available. Government extravagance and mismanagement led to corruption. The Credit Mobilier, a financial organization associated with the Union Pacific, made over $50,000,000 before the road was completed—one of the many scandals that rocked the Grant administration.

Despite the hastiness and inefficiency of their construction, the roads when completed were much in demand, and invariably they made a heavy contribution to the areas they served. They opened new and fertile sections of the American West, while older parts of America, bypassed in the westward rush, emerged from their isolation only when linked to the new commercial centers.

The new age of steel was characterized by specialization. As modern transportation and communication facilities opened up new markets, manufacturers began to concentrate on a single kind of product. With specialization came interchangeability of parts, mass production, and mass marketing—all of which increased efficiency of operation. By using time-saving and laborsaving techniques and by perfecting distribution methods, the most progressive manufacturers drastically cut their unit costs. Sometimes they passed on the saving to the customers, but more often they used the profit to combine and expand in their own field, hoping to drive out competitors and thereby enlarge their own markets.

For the tendency toward consolidation and monopoly was strong during the 19th century. It was a roughhouse game in which weaker players were

This telephone receiver is one of several that were exhibited and demonstrated by Alexander Graham Bell at the Philadelphia Exposition of 1876.

Thomas Edison had worked for 72 consecutive hours on his wax-cylinder phonograph when the photo was taken in 1888 from which this likeness was painted.

carried off the field with alarming frequency. The winners made no apologies. With some justification, they argued that the nation was the chief beneficiary of their efficiency, which brought inexpensive goods of high quality to the average household. They added that the evils of monopoly —if, indeed, there were evils—were a small price to pay for such material advancements. And it was perfectly true that their success, whatever its less desirable by-products, was due primarily to the application of initiative in a system of free enterprise. It

was, therefore, quite within the American tradition.

The results were spectacular. Giant industries sprouted, reaching heights of productivity that amazed the world and made Americans proud. The genius of the Yankee inventor and the semihumorous slogan "The difficult we do at once; the impossible takes a little longer" became a part of the American heritage. The conviction spread that in this land of "go-ahead," the industrial horn of plenty would ever refill itself. The nation was confident, cocky. It had found the

THE AMERICAN WORKINGMAN OF THE FUTURE.
When the Labor Agitators Have "Improved His Condition" Until He is Perfectly Satisfied With It.

In 1887, Puck *ridiculed the unions for trying to improve the lot of the workingman, showing him in exaggerated situations for which he is unprepared.*

key to industrial success; ahead lay economic paradise.

Two important things were wrong with the picture, however. First, the government machinery—federal, state, and local—of a traditionally agrarian nation was not geared to cope with the problems of an industrial society. *Laissez faire,* or "let alone," was still the guiding principle.

Government, it was believed, should stand in the background—an idle policeman awaiting a report of some lawbreaking before taking action.

The second trouble lay in the distribution system. All too often, manufactured goods failed to get into the hands of the intended users, and foodstuffs did not find their way from the farm to the hungry city workers.

There were enough railroads, warehouses, and telephone and telegraph facilities to keep the goods moving, but as the 19th century got older, the nation seemed to be suffering from a hardening of the economic arteries. To businessmen, whose capacity to understand the complexities of distribution had been outstripped by the speed of their country's commercial growth, the causes of the ailment were a mystery. Still, they were quick to object to suggestions that the federal government step in and try to effect a cure. There was, they believed, no cause for concern. As for the government, without major changes it was in no position to play such a part.

There were other troubles. From time to time, industry overproduced —or, as the manufacturers preferred to say—the nation underconsumed. Whichever it was, the results were industrial cramps and spasms. An unfavorable market almost always caused a shutdown of factories until demand picked up again. This brought extreme hardship to the workers, crowded as they were into their industrial ghettos.

Still, for a long time, ordinary people—like the tycoons themselves—did not want to go to any great length in search of a remedy. Few, rich or poor, questioned the theory that there was opportunity for all. With achievement measured in dollars, no one thought of condemning the Carnegies, the Rockefellers, or the Morgans; they were simply ordinary men who had gained fortune's favor. The common man felt that in this marvelous national lottery, his might be the next name called out.

The Robber Barons

The trouble with American financial success was that it was sometimes too successful. Ex-Ambassador Charles Francis Adams, returning from England in 1871, complained that the first five years after Appomattox "witnessed some of the most remarkable examples of organized lawlessness, under the forms of law, which mankind had yet had an opportunity to study." It struck him as wrong that one man could command hundreds of miles of railroads and another could have hundreds of millions of dollars. "In all this they have wielded a practical independence of control of both governments and of individuals," he wrote. By the end of the century, a great many Americans had begun, however unconsciously, to agree with him. To them, wealth was one thing, but excessive wealth seemed to warrant investigation. When money began to affect political developments or tilt the scales of justice, something had to be done.

But what? Opinions varied. A few reformers were ready to scrap capitalism; others, mainly the socialists, talked about major revisions. At the other extreme were men of means like Andrew Carnegie, who, seeing no reason for change at all, continued to preach the gospel of "work and save."

The system was right; if people did not become millionaires, the cause lay in something other than a deficiency in the system itself.

That argument did not satisfy all Americans. There appeared, late in the 19th century, an increasing amount of literature critical of capitalism—Edward Bellamy's novel *Looking Backward;* Henry George's immensely popular *Progress and Poverty;* Henry Demerest Lloyd's *Wealth Against Commonwealth.* To the distress of the wealthy, what a later age would call their public image was beginning to deteriorate. Some of them tried to ignore the talk. Others, disturbed by the insinuation that they were simply taking what they wanted, eased their consciences by giving it away. But most agreed that the outcries against them and capitalism were subversive.

Those who demanded that big business be regulated did not consider themselves subversive. They went on the theory that monopoly could be efficient but at the same time harmful to consumers. The emergence of trusts controlling large segments of the economy was of particular concern. Standard Oil, for example, accounted for 90% of the petroleum industry; the American Sugar Refining Company, about 85% of the sugar industry.

In answer to growing complaints, Congress, in 1890, passed the Sherman Antitrust Act prohibiting "combinations . . . in restraint of trade." It was loosely drawn: Nowhere did it define a trust or explain what restraint of trade meant. Senator Orville Platt of Connecticut frankly admitted, "The conduct of the Senate has not been in the line of honest preparation of a bill to prohibit and punish trusts . . . and the whole effort has been to get some bill headed 'A Bill To Punish Trusts' with which to go to the country." The truth of the Senator's statement was revealed during the 1890s, when the Supreme Court handed down decision after decision against those trying to enforce the law. Initially, most of the actual prosecutions were directed against labor unions—considered, in a business-minded society, "combinations" restraining trade. Thus, although the Sherman Act was intended to protect the laborer and the consumer from monopolistic power, it was for many years exercised for the opposite end.

Robber Barons on the defensive

Nevertheless, the industrialists did not go unregulated throughout the age of steel. Indeed, the Civil War was not many years past before they were stung by regulatory or tax laws passed by individual state legislatures. For relief, business quickly turned to the Supreme Court, traditionally conservative and always jealous of legislative powers. The immediate weapon used by corporation lawyers was that clause of the Fourteenth Amendment that says no state shall "deprive any person of life, liberty, or property, without due process of law." It was one of the reconstruction-era amendments, and most people assumed that the "person" referred to was the black citizen. Businessmen insisted, however, that a corporation was an entity, hence an individual or a person, and that the various states, through excessive taxation and regulation, were trying to take corporate property without due process.

At first, the courts upheld the state legislatures, but after about 15 years of trying, the corporations won their first big case before the high court: In the Minnesota Rate Case of 1889, the justices agreed that the action of a state legislature to reduce rail rates constituted a deprivation of property without due process. That broke the dam. During the next three decades, the Fourteenth Amendment was used nearly 800 times to protect corporations against hamstringing legislation.

Labor flexes its muscles

As society became more and more industrialized, business faced another challenge—organized labor, which wanted better working conditions and a larger share of the profits. Before the Civil War, nationwide labor unions had been almost nonexistent, and in the immediate postwar years, labor made scant progress. It had little power to enforce its demands.

When organized workers finally turned militant, employers called for

Eugene Debs and his American Railway Union were considered by the artist a threat to the nation's economy because of their strike for higher wages.

Federal cavalry clears the way for a train to pass through the American Railway Union's lines in Chicago, Illinois, during the Pullman strike that took place in June, 1894.

help, and it came—in the form of state or federal troops. But hard times, touched off by the panic of 1873, put workers in a fighting mood. By 1877, there were a number of strikes, principally against the railroads. Both the Baltimore & Ohio and the Pennsylvania were struck that year, and in both cases federal bayonets—provided by President Rutherford B. Hayes—were used to break up the rioting. The trouble spread to the Delaware, Lackawanna & Western, and as far west as Chicago.

The strikes of 1877 gained little for the railroad workers, but in the long view they benefited labor as a whole by demonstrating that it had fighting power. The Knights of Labor, founded in 1869, now took on new strength and prepared for future battles. By the middle 1880s, the Knights had 700,-000 members.

Then came trouble. A series of unsuccessful strikes discouraged a good many members, and in the spring of 1886, the violence erupted that was to put the whole labor movement, and the Knights in particular, in bad repute.

In May, a long strike against the McCormick Harvesting Machine Company in Chicago resulted in a riot. Police broke it up, and in Haymarket Square the next day, when workers returned to protest, someone threw a bomb that killed seven persons and injured 60 more. Although no one could positively identify the bomb thrower, a judge found eight "anarchists" guilty and sentenced seven of them to death. Four of the condemned were hanged, one committed suicide, and the other two had their sentences commuted to life imprisonment. Although the Knights of Labor were in no way responsible for the riot or its consequences, labor in general suffered, and the Knights ex-

perienced a serious decline. By 1890, their membership had dwindled to about 100,000.

Out of the wreckage of the Knights there arose the American Federation of Labor, led by Samuel Gompers, a member of Local No. 144 of the Cigar Makers' Union of New York City. The new organization was composed of a number of craft unions combined into one large federation, with a structure resembling that of the United States government. Each member un-

ion had complete power to deal with its employers, the federation itself merely acting as a national representative and co-ordinator.

Among the battles fought by the A.F.L., two stand out. The first was waged in 1892 in the Homestead, Pennsylvania, plant of the Carnegie Steel Company. There, some 300 Pinkerton detectives were hired to evict the strikers. The steelworkers fired upon the Pinkertons as they sailed up the Monongahela River toward the

829

plant. After a wild affray, the strike-breakers surrendered, were held prisoners of war for 24 hours, and then were run out of town. Henry Frick, in charge of Carnegie's operations at the time, called for help and promptly received it in the form of soldiers. Management broke the strike.

The second conflict grew out of a dispute between sleeping-car manufacturer George M. Pullman and his employees in the factory town of Pullman, Illinois. In 1894, management cut wages but continued to charge the same food prices at the company stores and the same rents for company houses. The American Railway Union under Eugene V. Debs came to the aid of the Pullman workers, and the disorder spread to all Western railroads using the company's cars. The railroads made management's familiar plea for federal assistance, and President Grover Cleveland gave it, over the heated protests of Governor John P. Altgeld of Illinois. It was another triumph for the industrialists, who knew that they had behind them a large body of American opinion and hence the administration at Washington, whether Democratic or Republican. It is small wonder that the supporters of organized labor found their uphill fight discouraging.

Modern America

Toward the end of the 19th century, a new American nation emerged—one whose characteristics sufficiently resembled those of the present day to be called "modern." Not only did manufacturers supply those who went forth to conquer what remained of the unsettled West, but they looked around the globe for new markets. It was a time of great urban growth, of a steady movement of people from the farm to the city. It was also a time when a man with real ability and a little luck could, as the popular Horatio Alger used to put it, "rise from the ranks" to great power and wealth. For thousands of young Americans who aspired to follow them up the ladder, the success of Carnegie, Rockefeller, and Morgan was a spine-tingling story.

But it was not written without a price. In the wild scramble to the top, some allowed their acquisitive instincts to dominate everything else, and the world came to think of all Americans as dollar chasers. In that chase there were many innocent casualties. Men worked at such a pace that health was endangered. Industrial slums proliferated. The end in sight was wealth, and the means became secondary.

By 1900, thoughtful persons had begun to look upon the warfare among the business titans with growing distaste. Angered by what they considered the apathy of most of their fellow citizens, a few of these men and women resolved to spread the gospel of reform. Their success paralleled David's victory over Goliath. But that story belongs to another era of history.

COVERDALE AND COLPITTS

MAKE WAY FOR
THE IRON HORSE!

In 1804, when canal boat and stagecoach were the accepted modes of travel, an Englishman built the world's first successful locomotive. Puffing at five miles an hour along a nine-mile track, it carried ore for an ironworks in Wales. By 1830, the idea had crossed the Atlantic, and a locomotive built in New York made the first passenger run in the United States. It could pull 50 passengers at 21 miles an hour. Canal and stagecoach men saw the handwriting on the wall: despite their dire warnings of exploding boilers on these steam monsters, the public took to the new contraption, and by the beginning of the Civil War, the nation had 31,246 miles of railroads. In addition, it had a new hero for the American boy—the brave engineer standing at the throttle of the *Fast Mail* as it thundered past, smoke belching and brass gleaming, with its hook out to seize the mail pouch (above).

MAKE WAY FOR THE IRON HORSE!

FROM COAST TO COAST

Inevitably, the demand arose for a coast-to-coast rail system. In 1862, Lincoln signed the Pacific Railroad Act, and two new companies were formed to undertake the construction job. The Central Pacific (above) started at Sacramento, and with a labor force made up largely of Chinese laborers, pushed east over the Rockies. The Union Pacific was to begin with existing railheads at Omaha and drive west. At last the great day came (right) when the two lines tied the country together.

MAKE WAY FOR THE IRON HORSE!

THE DRIVING
OF THE
GOLDEN SPIKE

The Civil War had created a labor shortage, so the Union Pacific made up the deficit by importing workmen from Ireland. As the two lines drew closer, friction grew between Irish and Chinese, and there were a number of brawls. In spite of them, the two lines were finally linked on May 10, 1869, at Promontory Summit, Utah. Assorted dignitaries were to drive the golden spike that made the final link, but the gentlemen could not handle a sledge hammer, and that job was done by a Union Pacific construction boss. The photograph (right) shows the actual event; the painting (above) is a fiction commissioned by Governor Leland Stanford of California, which shows the governor himself standing in the center of the tracks. Some of the others were not even alive.

THE ROADS GROW UP

The story of post-Civil War railroading is the story of little lines, some of which operated fewer than 100 miles of track, being absorbed into larger and more efficient systems. As the lines fought for business with blaring posters, big roads swallowed little ones and then fought among themselves until the biggest, like Cornelius Vanderbilt's New York Central, had acquired huge holdings.

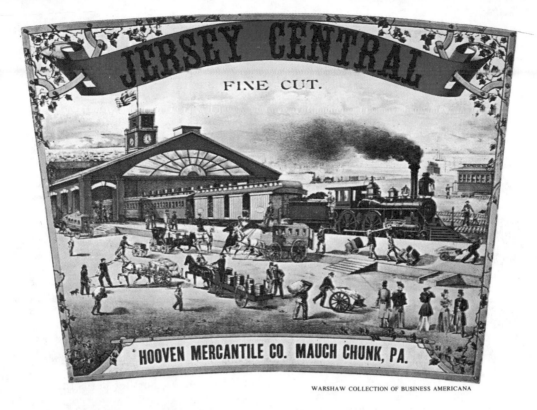

MAKE WAY FOR THE IRON HORSE!

TROUBLE
IN THE WEST

On the frontier, harsher perils than predatory financiers faced the railroads. Prairie fires might threaten the cars, and the still plentiful buffalo (above) could derail a train if stampeded. The Indians (below) did not care for the iron horse on their hunting grounds, and passengers often used their own firearms while waiting for the United States cavalry to come riding to the rescue.

COLLECTION OF A. HOWARD STEBBINS

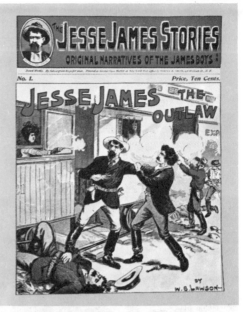

An even more serious threat than Indians was that posed by train robbers, whose crimes reached a peak in the 1870s. The James gang (below, seated, left to right, are Frank and Jesse; standing, cohorts Cole and Bob Younger) virtually became national heroes (right), with deeds celebrated in the Robin Hood tradition. Sympathy for the James boys was rife among small farmers, whose anger was directed against the railroads for charging them higher rates than the bigger shippers paid. In the end, the train robbers were recognized for what they were—common gunmen—and farmers turned to peaceable organizations like the Grange to put their plight before Congress.

RIDING ON THE ROADS

Railroad travel had come a long way from the bare wooden benches on which the early passengers had jolted. In 1864, the enterprising George Pullman began building his Pullman Palace Car (right) that even included comfortable sleeping accommodations. The station lunch counter (below) was replaced by the dining car, and trips became so safe that small children traveled alone (below, right). The very wealthy were transported in their own richly appointed private cars. The Pullman company produced at least 350 of these.

MAKE WAY FOR THE IRON HORSE!

THE HEYDAY OF THE HORSE

In the railroads' great days, the arrival of a train was a high point in the life of a town. Above, in the painting by E. L. Henry, the 9:45 a.m. *Accommodation* has just pulled into Stratford, Connecticut. The engine is a wood burner, as one can tell from the "balloon" smokestack; the engineer has decorated the headlight with a pair of antlers. The town has come to say good-bys, to meet arrivals, and simply to take a look at their most important link with the world.

GIFT FOR THE GRANGERS.

"I PAY FOR ALL."

FAITH,
HOPE,
CHARITY
FIDELITY

CHAPTER 29

AGRICULTURE, ADVERSITY, AND AGITATION

America has often been called the promised land. The promise is made up of many things: Political freedom, for one. Religious toleration, for another. And, of course, the opportunity for each man to follow his private dream and rise as high as his abilities will take him. But present-day Americans, especially those who are city-bred, may find it hard to realize how important a part of the promise was land itself. To an impoverished European peasant destined to live out his life tilling the soil of a wealthy landlord, or even to a New England farmer trying to scratch a livelihood out of a rocky hillside pasture, the rich and almost unbelievably abundant land west of the Mississippi seemed paradise indeed.

And it was so easy to own. Beginning with the Ordinance of 1785 and extending to the Homestead Act of 1862, the acquisition of farm sites steadily became easier. The Preemption Act of 1841 set the price of public land at $1.25 an acre and con-

The slogan under the main figure in this granger poster, "I Pay for All," gives the farmer's view of his place in the economy.

ferred upon the buyer the right to plant a crop and build a cabin on it even before it had been surveyed. Then, with the passage of the Homestead Act, any citizen could obtain a quarter section—160 acres—merely by paying nominal filing charges and living on it for five years. The words "free land" had a powerful effect upon prospective settlers: At the end of the Civil War, thousands of former soldiers and even greater numbers of nonveterans moved across the Missouri River to seek out new homes on the plains.

But 160 acres was not enough, particularly if the farmer also wanted to graze cattle on it. In 1877, Congress passed the Desert Land Act, offering homesteaders an additional section (640 acres) in exchange for a 25¢-an-acre filing fee and "conducting water upon the land." Buyers had three years to "prove up." Many stockmen, however, abused the government's generosity. They bought thousands of acres by means of a simple subterfuge: They put their cattle to graze on it for three years and told their cowboys to sprinkle a cupful of water here and there so the land would be "irrigated."

The wooded areas of the West Coast became the lumberman's paradise after passage of the 1878 Timber and Stone Act, under which land was sold cheaply.

Sometimes they carried the pretense further and put in some "ditches," but these were no more than plow furrows that ran up and down hills with no regard to the laws of gravity. Then, instead of proving up, the stockmen simply sold their land at a considerable profit to the first interested buyers.

Another government attempt to give away more land—although it did not help farmers much—was the Timber and Stone Act of 1878, under which a man could buy, for as little as $2.50 an acre, quarter sections of wooded, rocky land unfit for cultivation. West Coast lumbermen scoured the grogshops for hangers-on who would register their claims and then turn them over to the companies for logging. At first, the fee for such a service was $50, but soon it dropped until men could be found who would oblige for a glass of beer. By the 20th century, over 3,500,000 acres of valuable forest land were taken up under the law. But despite the fraudulent activities of stockmen and lumber interests, the settlement of the West by individual farmers went on.

The government, by repeatedly liberalizing the Homestead Act, set off the greatest land rush in the history of the country. The movement was so great during the 1870s that even the Mississippi Valley states lost population to the adjoining plains. This army of native settlers was joined by millions of immigrants, who, to claim land, needed only to declare their intention of becoming citizens.

Within a decade after the Civil War, some Easterners began to fear that the movement was too large and too fast.

No one listened to them. Even though the panic of 1873 had driven agricultural prices down 10% to 30%, the westward movement persisted. Free government land, or cheap railroad land, still was available in quantity. Hard times and savage competition had kept most railroad rates from rising and had even lowered some of them. The European markets still demanded grain in quantity. Money could still be made behind a plow.

Technological advances also sustained the migration westward. Improvements and recent inventions in farm machinery meant that more land could be worked by the average fam-

Two cowboys, in this painting by Charles Russell titled Come Out of There, *try to rope a stray cow that has wandered off with its calf down a gully.*

ily unit. Cyrus McCormick's reaper and John Deere's steel plow had been in general use since the Civil War, of course, but now, to join them in making life on the farm easier, came a rush of useful machines. Within a single President's term, that of Rutherford B. Hayes (1876–1880), the spring-tooth harrow, the twine binder, the centrifugal cream separator, and the gang plow were developed, and within a decade after that, Iowa corn growers were shucking and binding their crop mechanically. Cheaper land

and laborsaving devices had a dramatic effect. In the last three decades of the century, the number of acres under cultivation jumped from fewer than 500,000,000 to nearly 900,000,000. In the aggregate, farming was becoming big business.

Advances in milling methods also helped. In an earlier day, flour made from the hard kernels of spring wheat had been of low quality. Then came the invention of the roller process that successfully milled spring wheat—the hard, high-protein grain that grew

Pulled by 33 horses, this combine heads, threshes, and cleans the grain as it moves across a wheat field near Walla Walla, Washington, in 1902.

This homesteader is foraging ahead of his wagon, and with one bird in hand, he stands ready for whatever else might flush from the deep grass.

best across the northern part of the United States. Farmers poured into Minnesota, the Dakotas, and later, Montana. The nation's per-capita production of grain nearly doubled between 1860 and 1880, and America's milling capital moved westward from Rochester, New York, to Minneapolis.

The Western railroads were a tremendous stimulus to settlement. In this new age of steel, the old iron tracks gave way to heavier rails, and such advances as the Westinghouse air brake made trains out of what had once been unwieldy strings of cars. The result was a greater carrying capacity and higher speeds for the railroads, which soon began to penetrate virgin country.

Building in advance of settlement, laying down numerous feeders, or granger roads, the railroads beckoned the farmers westward and helped persuade them to stay by guaranteeing swift and efficient delivery of any and all crops they could grow.

It was an aggressive campaign. In thousands of newspaper advertisements, pamphlets, posters, and brochures, the railroads touted the new promised land. Papers as far away as Norway, Sweden, and Germany told how easily land could be had in the American West. In its first year, the Northern Pacific immigration bu-

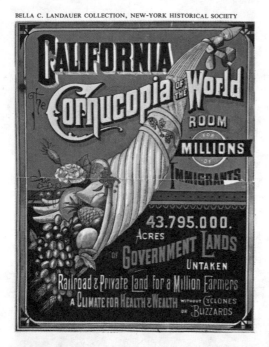

A poster designed to draw settlers to the State of California told of free land and opportunity, pointing out, at the end, that there were no cyclones or blizzards.

reau, established in 1874, sent out 25,-000 circulars and 25,000 booklets—one-fifth of them printed in German. By 1883, the Northern Pacific had 800 agents operating in the United Kingdom, 20 in London alone. Inquiries from would-be immigrants soared to 60,000 a year, and in reply over 2,500,000 pieces of literature were mailed.

Such literature painted the American West in glowing terms. Seed, it was said, produced crops of amazing size. Drought, loneliness, and Indians—the major enemies of the pioneer homesteader—were discreetly unmentioned. In an exaggerated passage, the Union Pacific praised the Platte Valley as "a flowery meadow of great fertility clothed in nutritious grasses, and watered by numerous streams." According to Burlington Railroad pamphlets, Western wheat farms produced 30 bushels to the acre, and cornfields 70 bushels. Crop samples and testimonial letters were sent to all parts of the world. Here was concrete evidence of a plowman's utopia, waiting only for the plow.

Growing pains

Free land, cheap transportation, and powerfully persuasive railroad advertising—all these helped flood the West with farmers. Although the land did not in every case live up to advance billing, it did in the aggregate yield more grain than America or Europe was prepared to eat. These enormous American crops, combined with mounting agricultural competition from Russia, Canada, Australia, and Argentina, glutted the world market and drove prices down. Corn that commanded 63¢ a bushel in this country during 1881 sold for only 28¢ in 1890. That year out in Kansas (where transportation charges had to be deducted), it was worth a mere 10¢ a bushel. During the 1880s, wheat averaged just above 70¢ a bushel, and the price of cotton had plummeted from 15¢ a pound to 8¢. Conditions became so bad that a Nebraska farmer was said to have shot his hogs, for he could neither sell them nor give them away. His plight seemed to support the national statistics; farming was losing out as a means of livelihood.

Why? The easy and apparently obvious explanation was overproduction. But that was hard for any farmer to understand. From the time of the first settlements, there had been—except for seasonal transportation stoppages—a steady market for farm produce. Despite the tremendous increase in crop production after the Civil War, there still were Easterners who did not have all the food they needed. As long as makers of clothes were underfed and producers of food were underclad, farmers believed that the term "overproduction" was meaningless. Quite reasonably they asked why Kansans were burning corn for fuel when laborers along the Atlantic seaboard were in need of groceries. They wondered if there were not some artificial barrier between producer and consumer. Were there not "certain influences at work, like thieves in

Immigrants traveling to their new homes in the West set up housekeeping and often spent their long and hard journey in a single railway coach.

the night," bent upon robbing the farmer of his labors? It seemed there were: The railroads.

Robber Barons on rails

The reputation of the Western roads fluctuated violently. When they had plunged across unsettled country, gambling that enough farmers would follow in their wake to make transportation profitable, they had been the darlings of the Western public. Their fabulously low rates, offered to farmers who wished to move their entire families onto a homestead, and even to excursionists who merely wanted to look over the Western farm lands, brought the warmest approval. Of course, all the time the railroads were receiving large land grants for laying tracks across the trans-Mississippi West, but the farmer did not begrudge them that privilege until he himself was faced with poverty and bankruptcy. Then he turned against the railroads and blamed them for his problems, just as he had blamed the Second Bank of the United States half a century earlier. The West's railroaders now became its villains.

When these corporate giants warred upon one another and lowered rates in competitive areas, they were inclined to recoup resultant losses by charging more in other Western areas where they had a monopoly. Overnight these new benefactors became criminals in the eyes of their agricultural customers. Some crops had to be moved as many as 2,000 miles to market, and the railroads did not try to hide the fact that they were charging all the traffic would bear. Angered farmers complained that when it cost one bushel of corn to send another bushel to market, it was more than they could afford.

To be fair, many of the roads were in a precarious financial position. Often they had been conceived in the belief that the creation of towns along the route and the resultant increase in the value of adjacent railroad lands would bring handsome profits. The towns themselves had become great railroad boosters. In the 1880s, one small Kansas town that served as headquarters for one road and was located on the principal route of another, voted bonds for still a third, tried to get a fourth to include it on its route, and appointed committees to search for still more roads.

In a good many instances this kind of promotion failed to bring the railroads the profits they had expected. Faced by declining revenues, their officials saw no recourse but to continue high rates. The farmers had no choice but to pay. Shippers complained, loudly, too, that short-haul rates were much higher than those for the long haul. It was hard for them to understand why, in the words of historian John D. Hicks, "wheat could actually be sent from Chicago to Liverpool for less than from certain points in Dakota to the Twin Cities."

Similarly, Dakota wheat growers were furious because they were re-

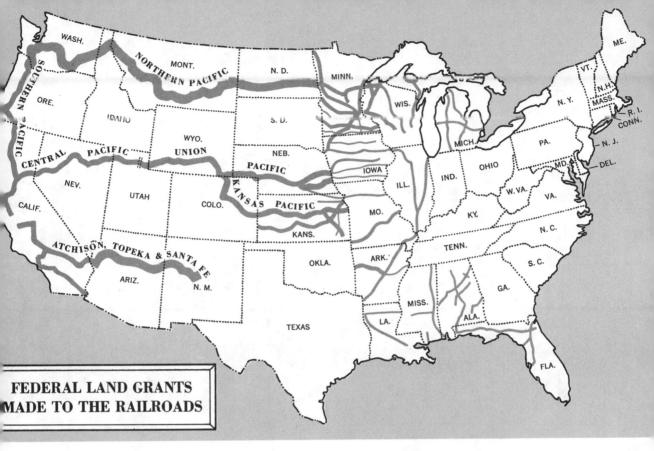

FEDERAL LAND GRANTS MADE TO THE RAILROADS

Approximate areas of federal land grants to the railroads are shown by the dark lines on the map. Part of the cost of building these railroads was met by selling some of this land to farmers who came to settle there.

quired to use railroad-owned elevators, where both loading and storage charges were assessed. To make matters even worse, elevator managers had a habit of "downgrading"—arbitrarily classifying the wheat as being of a lower grade, so they could buy it cheaper. The farmer was helpless. He could submit, or he could take his wheat home. As a rule he sold, but every time he did, his bitterness grew.

Prairie politics

Americans are a peaceful people, but if they are pushed around—or feel that they are being pushed around—they will get up and fight. In the latter years of the 19th century, this is exactly what farmers did.

During the 1870s, they rallied to the banner of the Patrons of Husbandry, organized in 1867 by a Bureau of Agriculture clerk named Oliver H. Kelley. By 1875, the Patrons had 800,-000 members in 20,000 granges, or local units. The Patrons organized hundreds of granger cooperatives, elevators, creameries, and warehouses, started farm-machinery factories, set up insurance companies for their membership, and originated the mail-order business—which, after Montgomery Ward was founded in 1872, would pass into other hands. All

The classroom of the schoolhouse in Edwardsville, Illinois, is used in the early 1870s by the local grange to hold its meetings and discussions.

these projects were aimed at lowering prices for the farmers, but this did not reach the root of their difficulty. A good many of them were still frustrated by the attitude of the courts and disappointed that the political power of the Grange was not greater or its representatives more aggressive. They were in an angry mood and wanted a fighting leadership.

In the National Farmers' Alliance, organized in 1880, they hoped they had the answer. Its main objectives were to seek more favorable railroad and tax legislation and to legalize Grange insurance companies. The father of the Alliance was Milton George, editor of the *Western Rural,*

a Chicago farm journal. Hard times during the early 1880s stimulated the movement and sharpened George's accusations against the railroads. By 1882, the Alliance was said to have 100,000 members; by 1890, hard times were so general in the rural West that over 1,000 new members were joining each week.

The local chapters of the Alliance made their presence felt. They were loud in their agitation for state regulation—if not outright ownership—of corporations, and they openly opposed absentee ownership of rural land. They demanded the establishment of agricultural subtreasuries—government warehouses where farmers could store their nonperishable products, receiving loans of up to 80% of the market value while holding their crops for more favorable prices. Within a single lifetime, this would no longer be considered a wild-eyed scheme. In the administrations of Woodrow Wilson and Franklin D. Roosevelt it would become reality.

Perhaps the most important political movement of the late '80s was the People's Party, commonly called the Populists. It was first organized in Kansas during the spring of 1890, and during the next two years, membership skyrocketed. By February of 1892, a national organization was formed. The views of the National Farmers' Alliance, if not its membership, became thoroughly identified with the new party. By campaign time in 1892, the agrarians were strong enough to enter national politics, and they did so with much fanfare.

At their first national nominating convention, held at Omaha, Nebraska,

With Carl Browne leading the parade on horseback, part of Jacob S. Coxey's army marches to Washington in 1894 to seek an end to unemployment.

that summer, the Populists made General James B. Weaver of Iowa their candidate for President. An able man, he had run for the Presidency on the Greenback ticket in 1880 and was fairly well known. An equally good choice as his running mate was ex-Confederate General James G. Field of Virginia. Former army officers like Grant, Hayes, and Garfield had dominated the Presidency since the Civil War, and the Populists hoped that a ticket with two of them—one from the North and one from the South—would have wide appeal.

The Populists declare themselves

The Populists' platform called for the free and unlimited coinage of silver, the adoption of the Alliance's subtreasury scheme, a graduated income tax, a postal savings bank, land reform, and government ownership of railroad, telegraph, and telephone facilities. They also asked for immigration restrictions and a shorter working day for industrial laborers. In an attempt to keep the party machinery out of the hands of professional politicians, the Populists approved a rule stating that no person holding a municipal, state, or federal office could sit or vote at any Populist convention. Many people vigorously approved.

The campaign of 1892 was more interesting and colorful than any had been for a long time. The Populists' major candidates made their appeal largely to the agricultural South and West, trying to acquire enough politi-

cal power to exercise a balance of control between the two older, traditional parties. Outspoken characters such as "Sockless Jerry" Simpson, Mary Elizabeth Lease, and Minnesota firebrand Ignatius Donnelly attracted wide attention. Mrs. Lease's advice to Kansas farmers to "raise less corn and more hell" was one of the memorable remarks of the campaign.

Thoroughly aroused, the Populists went to the polls in November, fiercely determined to make political history. They did. Democrat Grover Cleveland won the Presidency with 277 electoral votes to 145 for his Republican opponent, Benjamin Harrison, but Weaver polled over 1,000,000 popular votes and 22 electoral votes. His party carried Nevada, Idaho, Colorado, and Kansas; it elected governors in Colorado, Kansas, and North Dakota and sent 10 Representatives and five Senators to Washington. It was an impressive performance. Both major parties, not to mention the industrial East, could smell the smoke of this political prairie fire.

Success in 1892 generated considerable optimism among the Populists. They entered the off-year elections of 1894 with high hopes, but this time they were disappointed. Republicans recaptured Colorado and Idaho; there were reverses in Minnesota, the Dakotas, and Kansas; and in Iowa, General Weaver himself went down to defeat attempting to win a seat in the House of Representatives. But general distress brought on by the depression

GONE CRAZY.

An 1896 cartoon mocks the Democratic Party split between the sound-money men and the wild silverites, who are shown here leading the party into an abyss.

of 1893 sharpened the Populist appeal. Cleveland's attempt to stabilize the monetary situation by urging a repeal of the Sherman Silver Purchase Act produced some dark talk among Westerners. Even the Eastern businessmen, who breathed easier after the repeal, soon admitted that it had not cured

857

the financial ailment. Holders of silver certificates now surrendered them, but so many asked for gold in exchange that it began to appear that the government could not meet its obligations. Cleveland then made himself unpopular by borrowing gold from the banking house of J. P. Morgan. Out of the silver-producing West came cries of "betrayal" and "traitor."

The year 1894 was a time of discouragement for many Americans. Farm prices slumped to new lows and wages continued to fall. Bands of unemployed men formed themselves into "armies" led by "generals." In the spring of 1894, one of these restless groups—500 men under "General" Jacob S. Coxey—marched to Washington, where they chanted their demands outside the Capitol. The government responded by arresting the leaders for walking on the Capitol lawn.

In the West, where most farmers were always in debt, there was constant agitation that more money be put into circulation. This eventually crystallized into a demand for the free and unlimited coinage of silver at the ratio of 16 parts of silver to 1 of gold. A program of "free silver" was attractive not only to farmers but to silver miners, whose product had· fallen in price. As the campaign of 1896 drew near, the "silverites" and

the Populists were determined to join the "silver Democrats," in opposition to both the Republicans and the Cleveland "gold" Democrats. This political alliance would be the final attempt of the agrarians in the 19th century to gain their objectives at the polls.

At their nominating convention in 1896, the Republicans showed the

THE KEEPERS AT THE GATE.

same conservatism that, except for Cleveland's two terms, had carried them to victory ever since the Civil War. They nominated William McKinley of Ohio, best known for his protective tariff bill of 1890. In McKinley, "advance agent of prosperity," the Republicans hoped they had found a man who could stave off the Western uprising and put the Grand Old Party back in power. He and his party came out strongly for "sound money" as opposed to what they called "debased currency." Clearly the battle was to revolve around the money question.

The Democrats, divided between the gold and silver factions, bypassed

859

President Cleveland, the titular head of their party, and nominated silverite William Jennings Bryan, "the boy orator of the Platte." The young Nebraskan had set the convention afire with one of the greatest speeches in America's political history. Its memorable closing words were: "We will answer their demand for a gold standard by saying to them, 'You shall not press down upon the brow of labor this crown of thorns, you shall not crucify mankind upon a cross of gold.'" (See the special contribution on William Jennings Bryan at the end of this volume.)

The campaign was largely sectional. Bryan invaded the East—"enemy country," he called it—only briefly. He was more at home in the West, among his own people, and they responded to him. According to one legend, his appearance at Omaha drew such a large crowd that the auditorium overflowed. Not wishing to exclude anyone, Bryan agreed to speak outside, but the only thing he could find to stand on was a manure spreader. Without a moment's hesitation he mounted it, telling the crowd, "This is the first time I have ever spoken on a Republican platform." Earthy remarks like these had an enormous appeal to farmers, and Bryan's popularity soared.

The country had not seen such a campaign for decades and would not see anything like it again for many a year. Emotions ran especially high in the rural West. Kansas editor William Allen White compared the farmers' zeal to the fanaticism of the Crusaders. They drove their teams for miles through the night to hear pro-Bryan speakers in country schoolhouses. Bitter epithets were heaped upon Bryan in the East, and insurance companies hinted they would extend farm mortgages if McKinley were elected; but all this only strengthened the farmers' righteous resolve to vote for Bryan.

The mighty tide of rural resentment was not enough to put Bryan in the White House, however. McKinley, carrying the populous industrial states, won nearly 100 more electoral votes than the Westerner, even though the popular vote was closer—7,035,638 to 6,467,946. One Eastern religious magazine suggested the relief felt in some circles when it said, "Praise the Lord: The cause of National honor and righteousness has triumphed. The leaders of the forces of Free Silver and Repudiation, anarchy and class hatred have been overthrown, and their unrighteous cause is lost forever."

The election amply proved that the industrial world could hurl back the agrarian forces, no matter how great their anger or how solid their political organization. Westerners and Southerners had reason to be discouraged, but their children would live to see many of the Populist dreams come true when another era of hard times gave birth to Franklin D. Roosevelt's New Deal. That, however, would take a generation of waiting.

THE ROBBER BARONS

The name did not come into use until 1934, when Matthew Josephson coined it for the title of a book, but it is now part of the language. The Robber Barons were the great men of finance in late 19th-century America—famous men like the Vanderbilts, Carnegie, Morgan, and Rockefeller—but there were many other businessmen, the names of whom are not so famous, who expressed the new vitality that came into the country as the Industrial Revolution pervaded America during and after the Civil War. There was unleashed a new pioneer spirit, a certain recklessness and lawlessness, and a powerful creative talent—all centered around the single idea of accumulating as much money as possible. These men seemed to feel themselves free to operate as they wanted, the only standard being financial success. In this sense they represent better than any other single group the dynamic, imaginative, and often reckless power of the American economic system. It is to these men that part of America's economic greatness is traced. (In the cartoon, Vanderbilt, Gould, Field, and others divide the transportation profits in New York, with the suggestion that they might purchase Europe.)

THE VANDERBILTS

CORNELIUS VANDERBILT

WILLIAM H. VANDERBILT

Cornelius Vanderbilt, known as the Commodore because of his control of the ferry lines around New York City, was one of the first captains of industry, but it was not until he was 68, with a fortune of $11,000,000, that he began the period of his greatest success. It was at this time that he invested in railroads, bringing into existence the great New York Central. His method was to buy a railroad, improve it without spending too much money, consolidate it with other railroads to cut expenses, increase the value of the stock (sometimes by watering), and make it pay higher dividends.

One of his most difficult financial battles was over control of the Erie Railroad. It was a fracas in which Vanderbilt faced Jay Gould and James Fisk, who had taken as their cohort Daniel Drew. The story of the Erie thrown among these rivals is one of the tricks in financial legerdemain. The ending found Gould, Fisk, and Drew in a hotel in Jersey City, New Jersey, having sold illegal stock to Vanderbilt, and the Commodore in New York, throwing out injunctions for their arrest that could not be served. Finally, in 1868, they had to come to terms with Vanderbilt, but they also received their share of stock in the Erie.

William H. Vanderbilt was the Commodore's plain, stout son, who, late in life, after being a farmer on Staten Island, surprised people by turning into a brilliant, penny-pinching president of the New York Central. His giant figure in the cartoon, with Gould and Cyrus Field on his legs, shows the control he exercised over the transportation world of New York, including even the municipal transport in which Field was involved.

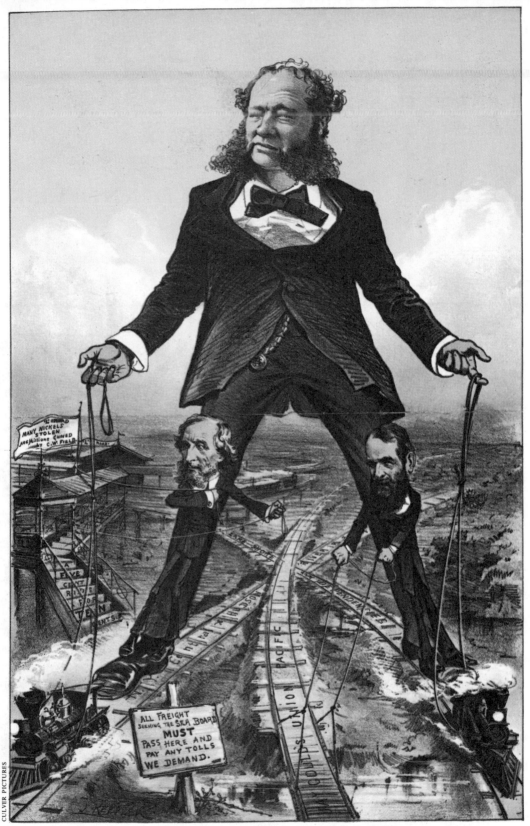

THE MODERN COLOSSUS OF (RAIL) ROADS.

863

JAY GOULD

GOULD AND FISK

JAY GOULD'S PRIVATE BOWLING ALLEY.

WONDERFUL TOUR DE FORCE,

RFORMED "ON THE BEACH AT LONG BRANCH," BY PROFESSOR JAMES FISK, JR. THE GREAT AMERICAN ATHLETE.

JAMES FISK

Jay Gould, silent and continually nervous, has been described as the most ruthless man on Wall Street. There was nothing about his personality to suggest that James Fisk become his partner. Fisk was a gregarious man, a loud and lavish spender. Yet he was also a sly businessman with great energy, and Gould found him a perfect foil.

One of the most incredible moves by any of the big financiers was made by Gould and Fisk in 1869 when they tried to take over the gold market of the country. The two worked with speed and stealth, moving right up to Abel Corbin, a lobbyist who was married to Grant's sister and had influence in the White House. They bought as much gold as they could get their hands on, hoping to corner the market. Their great day came on September 24—now known as Black Friday—when the market price of gold shot up at their bidding and it required government intervention to stop the panic. Hundreds of men on Wall Street claimed they had been ruined, but Gould and Fisk sold their gold before the market fell. The investigation made it clear that the blame went so high (even as high as the White House, was Fisk's unjustifiable implication) that it was difficult to make anyone responsible. These two had kept themselves in the clear. Not an order for the purchase of gold was ever made in their own names; the orders were all made in the names of their two bankrupt brokers.

"SHE'S MY DAISY."

"She's as sweet as sugar candy
And she's very fond of Andy."

CARNEGIE

Son of an immigrant labor leader from Scotland; telegraph boy who supported his family when work was short in America; avid reader of Robert Burns and Shakespeare; founder of over 2,800 libraries; ruthless businessman who became, some said, the world's richest—this unusual combination of background, ability, and character was Andrew Carnegie.

His name is now synonymous with philanthropy, but in his day it was not so kindly considered. Then it was linked with steel and money, as the cartoon indicates. An incident in which he played an important part is, oddly, one that he did not directly participate in—the steel strike in 1892 at his Homestead, Pennsylvania, plant. The strike was provoked by Henry Frick, president of Carnegie's steel company, but it had the full approval of the master. Frick wanted less union interference and lower wages for the workers. When it was time for their new contract, he arranged for steel orders to go to another plant, hired non-union men, and brought 300 Pinkerton guards to Homestead to keep the regular workers out until they agreed to his terms. On July 6, the union men and the guards met in a bloody battle in which 13 died. The mobs ruled for five days before the state militia came, but the strike was not over until November 21. A telegram was sent to Carnegie, who had remained in Europe, not wishing to return. His short, joyous answer to Frick was "Congratulations all around—life worth living again—how pretty Italia."

MORGAN

J. PIERPONT MORGAN, UNLIK
This Stirring American, Having Gaine

John Pierpont Morgan was involved in the business affairs of many of the Robber Barons, and he usually handled their chaotic financial activities with dignified authority. In part, this authority had to do with his appearance, which was awesome, but it also was the result of his background. He was born into a banking family, and he turned what his father left him into a

great fortune. This gave him a natural, easy assurance in comparison to men like Gould and Fisk, whose recent acquisition of money made them aggressive or showy. But Morgan was no less of a financial operator. His methods and power were feared and respected by Wall Street, making him one of the most influential and dominant figures in America.

...EXANDER THE GREAT, HAS MORE WORLDS TO CONQUER.
...trol of Our Railroads and Steel Business, is Reaching for the Shipping of the Universe.

His greatest success was in forming the United States Steel Corporation. By 1900, Carnegie wanted to devote more time to philanthropic and social interests, but when Morgan first suggested that he sell his steel holdings, Carnegie hesitated. He was reluctant to lose his share of the great American steel industry, but he finally agreed to sell. Carnegie's companies cost Morgan $492,000,000, and he made them, with several other companies, the basis of a huge steel trust that was capitalized at $1,404,000,000, thus beginning the era of the supertrust in American business.

When he died in 1913, Morgan left one of the world's richest banking houses— and to the Metropolitan Museum, one of the country's finest private art collections.

ROCKEFELLER

UNCLE JOHN

The face of John D. Rockefeller reveals much of his character. He was determined and methodical, devoting his attention to little besides business. When he did something, it was done precisely.

His purpose was always to buy at the lowest price and sell at the greatest profit. He was able to price his oil lower than that of his competitors by demanding and getting rebates from the railroads that carried it. He then reasoned that if he had control of the refining of oil, he could dominate the market and regulate the price of oil, keeping his profits high. His first try at monopolizing the market was thwarted by independent oil producers, but this did not stop him. He undersold his competitors until, by 1878, he controlled perhaps 80% or 90% of the nation's pipelines and refineries. By 1882, he was directing all the companies affiliated with Standard Oil through a group of nine trustees who set the price and the production quotas.

As the cartoons show, the public did not look kindly on the methods of this stern man. At the left he has become Uncle Sam, with his own eagle—Senator Nelson W. Aldrich, a strong supporter. Below, the sign expresses a 1903 attitude toward the Rockefeller philanthropies.

The son of an Episcopal minister, Edward H. Harriman became a sharp speculator in railroads. At 21 he had made $3,000 and bought a seat on the Stock Exchange; by 35 he owned his first railroad; and at 49 he took over the Union Pacific, which had never recovered from Jay Gould's manipulations. He put $25,000,000 into it, and two and a half years later the road declared a dividend. Harriman then used his credit to buy other lines, and eventually he became owner of 46% of the Southern Pacific.

An attempt to take over the Chicago, Burlington & Quincy Railroad brought him into conflict with James J. Hill, the railroad master of the Northwest. Hill wanted the Burlington, as it would give him a line into Chicago and expand his railroad empire, which then consisted of the Great Northern and the Northern Pacific. Harriman did not want Hill competing with his Union Pacific. Hill went into battle with the backing of J. P. Morgan. Behind Harriman was Rockefeller. In the first round, in 1901, Hill won the Burlington by buying stock control and selling it to his Northern Pacific. But Harriman was not to be stopped. He began secretly buying Northern Pacific shares, planning in this way to control the Burlington that it owned. When Hill and Morgan discovered what was happening, they tried to counter by buying all the Northern Pacific shares on the market. This skyrocketed the price and threw the market into a panic. Finally, Morgan offered peace by creating a holding company for Hill's railroads, shares of which were owned by both sides. Harriman's cleverness and perseverance had won him a voice in the Burlington, but Hill, who was made the chairman of the new company, still directed policy.

Harriman died in 1909 at the height of his career. The cartoon gives an indication of the scope of his power in this country. He did not dominate Hill, Morgan, and Gould, as the cartoon implies, but this small, shrewd businessman could make all of them jump when he wanted.

HARRIMAN AND HILL

CULVER PICTURES

872

EDWARD H. HARRIMAN   JAMES J. HILL

MR. HARRIMAN'S PLANS FOR REORGANIZING THE RAILWAYS OF THE COUNTRY

873

TRY YOUR STRENGTH, GENTS!

THE HARDER YOU HIT IT, THE HIGHER IT GOES.

CHAPTER 30

THE POLITICS
OF ECONOMIC GROWTH

The growth of the Populist Party was proof that the unprecedented burgeoning of industry in post-Civil War America had left deep pockets of resentment among the populace. More aggravating still, to the vast bulk of 19th-century Americans, were the dishonesty and corruption of so many men who held or sought public office. In 1873, what one newspaperman called "the creeping, crawling things beneath the surface" of the Grant administration began to come to light. Even the solidly entrenched Republican Party could not ignore the influence-peddling, the bribetaking, and the use of high office for private gain that brought the administration of the well-meaning soldier-President into disrepute.

In a sense, the turning point of the reform movement came on July 2, 1881, at the Washington railroad station, when a disappointed office seeker named Charles J. Guiteau drew a revolver and shot the President of the United States, James A. Garfield.

A Puck *cartoonist attacks the powerful trusts as hitting the consumer with high tariffs to make their profits greater.*

One of the bullets hit the President's arm, but the other lodged in his spine, and after lingering for 79 days, he died. Following a highly publicized trial, at which the public fought for seats, the assassin was pronounced guilty and was hanged.

Although the cry for civil-service reform now became much louder, it was not altogether new. Indeed, complaints about the spoils system dated back to the administration of George Washington. Inevitably, as political parties expanded dramatically, beginning with the Jackson era, preferment came to be used increasingly to discipline party members or to attract new ones. Then, during Andrew Johnson's bitter struggle with Congress after the Civil War, the use of patronage as a political weapon became alarmingly common.

When Grant came to the Presidency, reformers renewed their efforts. In his second annual message, the President tried to persuade Congress to enact legislation governing the manner in which appointments were made. Given an appropriation of $25,000 to study the matter, Grant at once appointed an advisory committee headed by George William Curtis, the scholarly editor of *Harper's Weekly*.

The report that the Curtis committee submitted after 10 months of study must have jarred Grant. It charged, among other things, that "The business of the nation, the legislation of Congress, the duties of the departments are all subordinated to the distribution of what is well called the spoils. No one escapes. President, Secretaries, Senators, Representatives are pertinaciously dogged and besought on the one hand to appoint and on the other to retain subordinates. The great officers of the government are constrained to become mere office brokers." Although Curtis was applauded for his frankness, there was no sudden turn toward reform.

But an articulate group of reformers fought on. In 1872, some of them,

CULVER PICTURES

A MODEL OFFICE-SEEKER.

The face of disappointed office seeker Charles J. Guiteau, Garfield's assassin, was used in this cartoon to comment on a spoils system that was a public disgrace.

876

led by Missouri Senator Carl Schurz and a handful of influential Congressmen and newspaper editors, bolted the G.O.P. to form the Liberal Republican Party, with reform of the civil service its principal platform plank. The party's charge that "The civil service of the government has become a mere instrument of partisan tyranny and personal ambition, and an object of selfish greed" failed to arouse the voters enough to elect the Liberal Republicans' Presidential candidate, Horace Greeley.

Grant's two terms, during which the odor of scandal had become overpowering, had thoroughly disillusioned the electorate, and all major parties advocated reform in 1876. Presumably, no matter which won, the voter was promised some improvement.

The victor, Republican Rutherford B. Hayes, appeared to be one of those who took his party's platform seriously. Somewhat to the disappointment of old-guard Republicans, he expressed the belief that "party leaders should have no more influence in the matter of appointments than any other equally respectable citizens." He frowned upon the practice of levying political assessments upon political appointees. Even more disconcerting to those who favored business as usual was the manner in which Hayes struck out at the spoils system, particularly in New York. Senator Roscoe Conkling became highly incensed at this invasion of his territory. With heavy

Shot on July 2, 1881, four months after becoming President, Republican James A. Garfield had no time to prove his abilities.

irony he said, "When Dr. Johnson defined patriotism as the last refuge of a scoundrel, he ignored the enormous possibilities of the word 'reform.'"

As far as political integrity was concerned, Hayes' administration was a notable improvement over Grant's, but no lasting reforms were initiated. It took the assassination of Hayes' successor, Garfield, to bring matters

877

Claiming a tradition from three great Presidents, the Democratic Party in 1884 nominated Cleveland and Hendricks and won for the first time in 24 years.

to a head. The Republicans, frightened into action, voted for a Democratic bill presented by Senator George H. Pendleton of Ohio. The Pendleton Act, which became law early in 1883, during the administration of Chester A. Arthur, provided for a Civil Service Commission and for a classified service among a limited number of government employees. Competitive examinations henceforth were to be the basis for certain appointments.

The new law had an early test. In 1885, two years after it was passed, the Democrats swept into office. Like every winning party, they had political debts to pay. Moreover, there had not been a Democratic President since Buchanan left office in 1861; the faithful had been awaiting this victory for 24 years. In anticipation, its fruits seemed sweet.

But the new President, Grover Cleveland, was a well-known reformer whose beliefs threatened to stand in the way of the usual handouts. As it happened, Democratic Party workers need not have been concerned: Within a short time, 90% of those whose jobs depended on Presidential appointment were removed to make way for the victors; almost all of the fourth-class postmasters, for example, were let out. There were loud cries from the reformers about broken promises and the failure of the civil service law, but the critics overlooked one important fact. Less than 7% of officials already under civil service had lost their jobs, and before Cleveland left office, he had brought a new group of federal employees—those in the railroad mail service—under the protection of the Pendleton Act. In succeeding administrations the practice of generously distributing patronage continued, but as time passed, the growth of the civil service was steady and the desirability of further reforming it was unquestioned.

A tax called the tariff

Demands for tariff reform made up another strident chorus in the chant of mounting dissatisfaction over the economic situation. Earlier in the century, the tariff had been the subject of much complaint from the agricultural South; now the West took up the cause as a part of its crusade against Northeastern capital. Manufacturing interests, more powerful than at any previous time in American history, fought back fiercely. High protective tariffs not only assured them a steady profit but compensated for any wastefulness or inefficiency on their part. The leaders of organized labor, fearing the effect of cheap foreign imports on the jobs of their members, joined the fight. Users of manufactured goods, however, and particularly farmers, charged that the tariff simply amounted to another tax upon the products they wanted to buy.

For the post-Civil War generation, the tariff question dated back to the Morrill Tariff of 1861, whose schedules were steadily increased during the war. Any effort to reduce them met stiff opposition from war-born industries, whose owners argued that they could not survive without government protection.

The first postwar tariff reduction that amounted to anything came in 1872, but the financial panic of the following year cut revenues so drastically that by 1875 the schedules were again raised. By the early 1880s, however, exports and imports rose sharply, partly because of the completion of the transcontinental railroads. The federal treasury had a surplus of approximately $100,000,000, and as the tariff was to a large degree responsible, demands for tariff reduction seemed only right. The efforts of Congress in that direction were disappointing: Rates were lowered only about 4% over all, and those industries whose spokesmen complained vigorously enough managed to escape any hurtful changes.

In 1887, under the first Democratic President since before the Civil War, the tariff question was thrown squarely into the political ring. When Grover Cleveland, in his annual message to Congress that year, recommended a tariff reduction, the Democrats openly supported him. The election of 1888, it appeared, would turn upon the tariff issue.

The Republicans won with Benjamin Harrison, and they interpreted the victory as a mandate to continue the high tariff. The result was even more protection in the McKinley Tariff of 1890. Two years later, the voters strongly suggested that they did not approve the upward revision: They returned Cleveland to the White House. It now appeared that the Democrats had a mandate to lower the tariff. Their response was disheartening to those who had hope for reduction. In the Wilson Tariff of 1894, the rates on some imports were lowered, but those on others were raised, nullifying the effect of any downward trend. With the return of the Republicans to power in 1897, there followed the highly protective Dingley Tariff, which raised duties

to an average level of 57%. Thus, by the end of the century, low-tariff advocates and those who charged the protectionists with supporting monopoly could claim no progress. Industry had gained another victory. For the moment, at least, reformers could do little but lament bitterly and husband their strength for the future.

Silver vs. gold

A reform issue that rivaled the tariff question during the late 19th century revolved around a subject that has always caused arguments—money. From the close of the Civil War to the election of 1896, the "Battle of the Standards" drew the attention of increasing numbers of Americans. Simply explained, it was a contest between those who wanted an inflated currency and those who preferred a "tight money" policy.

During the early post-Civil War years, the nation's rapid economic development made serious demands upon its financial resources. American railroad mileage doubled in less than a decade; as a result, vast new areas were opened to settlement. Enormous amounts of money were required to finance the myriad new communities, and when currency appeared to be in short supply, the government was charged with failure to provide enough of it—or with adopting outright deflationary policies.

Westerners especially were incensed at the government's reluctance to encourage what Eastern bankers called

DOCTOR CLEVELAND'S PATIENTS.

Uncle Sam (*to* Civil Service Reform).—Don't cry, my child, he'll look after you presently.   Your brother needs attention more than you do.

In this cartoon, Cleveland is pictured as a sensible man who will treat the ills of the war tariffs before looking at the need for civil-service reform.

inflation. During and after the Civil War, some $400,000,000 in legal-tender notes, called "greenbacks" or "Lincoln skins," had circulated without metallic backing. In 1868, when the amount of these bills outstanding was reduced to $356,000, there were complaints from those who wanted the currency expanded rather than contracted. In 1874, Congress authorized an increase to $400,000,000, but, to the dismay of the expansionists, President Grant vetoed the bill. In the Northeast he was, writes Matthew Josephson, "for a second time acknowledged . . . as the savior of his country." The farmers disagreed; in the Congressional elections

881

After the Civil War, the federal treasury accumulated a surplus, mostly the result of the tariffs voted in during the war. The businessman wanted tariff protection continued as it gave him greater profits, but

THE OPENING OF THE

TARIFF MONSTER.— Here I am again!

Keppler

CONGRESSIONAL SESSION.

What are you going to do with me?

the users of imported goods objected because they had to pay higher prices. As this cartoon implies, the surplus and the tariff were a bugbear that appeared before every new session of Congress.

of 1878, the Greenback Party's candidates polled 1,060,000 votes.

The Greenbackers had strong allies in the free-silver advocates. In 1792, the nation's first Secretary of the Treasury, Alexander Hamilton, had suggested the free and unlimited coinage of both gold and silver at the value ratio of 15 to 1. In 1834, during Jackson's second term, the ratio was adjusted to 16 to 1. The system worked well for the rest of the century; whenever any commodity is scarce, its price will be high, and silver, not being produced in any great quantity, could be sold on the open market at such a good price that there was no great demand to have it coined.

By 1873, Congress, noting that only around 8,000,000 silver dollars had been minted since George Washington's administration, dropped that item from its coinage list. No one objected. During the late 1870s, however, the production of silver suddenly rose sharply, which meant that its value plummeted; the unprotested action of Congress in 1873 suddenly became "the crime of '73." The mountain states, whose economy leaned heavily upon silver mining, cried out loudly. Farmers, perennially in debt, saw in the free and unlimited coinage of silver the inflation and expansion of circulating media they had wanted for so long. They joined the protest. It was this alliance that made the money question political dynamite.

To meet the complaints, Richard P. Bland, a Missouri Representative, and Senator William B. Allison of Iowa sponsored a bill directing the Secretary of the Treasury to buy at least $2,000,000 worth of silver (but not more than $4,000,000 worth) per month to be coined into silver dollars. President Hayes vetoed the bill, but in the spring of 1878, it was passed over his veto. The legislation, aimed at satisfying Westerners and all others who supported currency expansion, failed to halt the falling price of silver or to produce any marked inflation of the economy.

Meanwhile, instead of issuing more greenbacks, the Republicans promised to resume the payment of specie, or hard money, for any outstanding paper notes. "Resumption," which began on January 1, 1879, meant that paper and metallic money would have the same value to the users. In the face of cries from the proponents of inflation that resumption would mean falling prices and shrinking buying power, gold and greenbacks were put on a par with each other, and after nearly two decades, the nation returned to a currency based upon metallic value. Owners of bonds and those living on fixed incomes welcomed the reappearance of "sound money." But the farmers thought they had been betrayed.

A marked economic improvement temporarily quieted Westerners. The year 1879 produced a bumper farm crop, and it was sold for record prices —a situation that had a remarkable effect upon the voters. Republican candidates swept into office in states formerly commanded by Greenbackers. So complete was the vindication of Hayes' administration that in 1880 neither party put forward any demands for free silver or inflated money.

The respite was fairly short. Hard times returned in the mid-1880s, driving agricultural prices to new lows. At the same time, the soaring production of silver depressed its price catastrophically.

In 1889 and 1890, six new states —North and South Dakota, Montana, Washington, Idaho, and Wyoming—entered the Union. All relied heavily upon either agriculture or mining, and the appearance of their representatives in Congress renewed the pressure for easy money. Eastern Republicans had not changed their minds on the subject, but they had a pet project of their own—a new tariff bill that was before Congress. The situation was ripe for a horse trade. Westerners were persuaded to vote for the McKinley Tariff of 1890; in return, Easterners reluctantly supported the Sherman Silver Purchase Act.

The Sherman Act provided that the government should buy 4,500,000 ounces of silver each month, paying the market price in treasury notes. It was no more successful than the Bland-Allison Act. Democrats opposed it on the ground that it was only a palliative, not a cure. The goldbugs sneered at it as evidence that the case for silver was hopeless. Diehard silverites condemned it as a weak

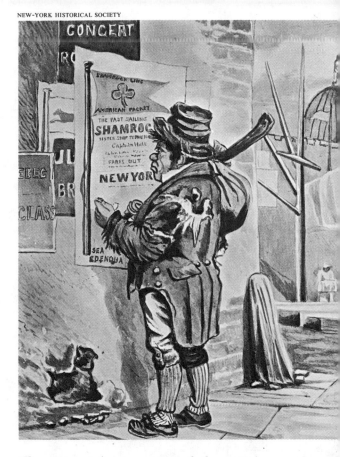

The cartoonist's stereotype of the native Irishman shows him in Dublin reading steamship notices promoting immigration.

compromise and a far cry from free and unlimited coinage. The law was in force only three years, during which approximately $156,000,000 worth of silver was bought. It was enough to stimulate some inflation, but not enough to raise farm prices appreciably. Cleveland's sponsorship of the successful effort to repeal the act brought praise from the creditor East and howls of outrage from the debtor West. His action also split the Democratic Party and threw the mon-

St. Patrick's Day was publicly celebrated as early as 1737 in Boston and 1762 in New York. Above, the 1874 New York parade marches through Union Square.

ey question squarely into the political ring, where it was snatched up by William Jennings Bryan and used as a principal weapon in his memorable, if unsuccessful, campaign of 1896.

"Give me your tired, your poor"

While industry was shooting up from infant to giant, while the West was being won, and while the country was convulsed by the inevitable growing pains, a revolution was under way. Beginning a few years before the Civil War, when the potato crop suddenly failed in Ireland, wave after wave of immigrants from Europe began landing at ports on the Eastern seaboard, drawn by the opportunity to begin life anew in a land of promise. Between 1865 and the century's end, almost 14,000,000 foreigners would arrive.

At first, native-born Americans, a naturally hospitable people whose own ancestors, after all, had been immigrants, welcomed the newcomers. Although it was written much later, Emma Lazarus' poem inscribed on the base of the Statue of Liberty proudly expressed their feelings:

Give me your tired, your poor,
Your huddled masses yearning to
breathe free . . .

And the newcomers were useful. They built the country's roads and canals, pushed the railroads westward, and fought—on both sides—in the Civil War. They did the dirty, backbreaking jobs in mine and mill without which the industrial boom would not have been possible.

Their coming had not, it is true, been entirely free of opposition. Even before the Civil War, the Irish in Boston and Philadelphia had seen their convents and churches burned, and the Know-Nothing Party, based on anti-Catholicism and anti-foreignism, had nearly captured the Presidency. But by the 1870s and 1880s, such mindless prejudice against the Irish and the other northern Europeans—chiefly Germans and Scandinavians—who made up the early waves of immigrants had largely subsided.

The newer immigrants who followed them in a stream that seemed to have no end were from the poorer, more crowded lands of southern and eastern Europe. They were less susceptible of assimilation, it appeared; they tended to cling longer to their "foreign" ways. They crowded into the slums of Eastern cities, where, without resources, they were forced into sweatshops, with all the evils attendant upon them. Furthermore, their coming coincided with hard times, dramatized by the panics of 1873 and 1893. The day of free land in the West, which had absorbed so many of the earlier immigrants, was nearly over. Jobs were scarce in depression years, and American labor was jealous to protect those there were.

Full cooperation for a campaign to stop the entry of immigrants came from the American Protective Association, founded in the Midwest in 1887. Although it was essentially anti-Catholic in purpose, it received much support from American workers who resented the competition from southern Europeans poorer than they and therefore willing to work for less. Soon after the turn of the century, the revived Ku Klux Klan, featuring 100% Americanism, would provide additional strength to the movement.

Until the late 19th century, there had been no federal legislation aimed at control of immigration. Such regulation as there was came from the states. Then, in 1876, the United States Supreme Court handed down a decision that control must be national in character. Congress was moved to act, albeit slowly. While it pondered —some six years—nearly 2,000,000 more immigrants were admitted. Californians were particularly insistent that action be taken to stop the immigration of Chinese—which they themselves had begun by importing coolie laborers to build the Central Pacific.

The first federal immigration law was passed in 1882. Simple and brief,

This Italian family was photographed at Ellis Island in 1905 as it awaited examination by the immigration authorities.

it provided that each immigrant pay a head tax of 50¢, that the newcomers be protected against fraud and loss of their possessions upon arrival, and that all paupers, convicts, and mental defectives be excluded. The Secretary of the Treasury was empowered to make arrangements with various states for the detention of undesirables. The law was neither comprehensive nor carefully drawn, but it did establish the principle of "selection by rejection" that was to be used repeatedly until the vastly more restrictive "quota law" of 1924 virtually slammed the door shut.

Meanwhile, demands for a further tightening of regulations continued. The government responded, in 1891, with the passage of a new Federal Immigration Act, designed to bar still more would-be Americans. More classes were excluded, and steamship lines were held responsible for keeping off their vessels any persons whom the law would inevitably bar from admission once they arrived. The lines insisted they could not comply, but they managed; eventually less than 1% of those they carried were rejected. Further changes in the law excluded more groups, but strict enforcement was virtually impossible.

Restricting immigration (and in the case of the Orientals, barring an entire race) bespoke a fundamental change in national attitudes. The change coincided roughly with the closing of the frontier, suggesting for the first time that Americans had

UNCLE SAM PERSPIRES AT HIS GROWING JOB.
He Finds Turning the Crank of the Assimilation Mill is Taxing His Strength to the Utmost.

Uncle Sam is seen by the cartoonist as sweating over his backbreaking task of turning the newly arrived immigrants on Ellis Island into American citizens.

some doubt as to the illimitability of their land. The desire to shut off the "new immigration," whose source was southern European and hence Latin, was based on old feelings about the desirability of Teutonic blood, and it brought to life the cult of American nativism, dormant since Know-Nothing days.

The immigration laws ignored at least two basic realities—first, the eagerness of most of the newcomers to become good Americans and, second, the rich cultural heritage that many of them brought to the New World. No small part of America's leading musicians, scientists, inventors, scholars, and businessmen were once humble immigrants, and the country would have been much poorer without their contributions.

The fear, during World War I, that these "hyphenated Americans" (principally the German-Americans) would be disloyal to their country of adoption proved unfounded.

All these movements toward reform—of the civil service, the tariff, the monetary system, and the immigration laws—were indications that America's rapid economic growth after the Civil War had been unplanned and uneven and that the government was needed to give a guiding hand. The architects of the new industrialism, who held that their good works were not fully appreciated, believed the government was overplaying its constitutional role. The debate would continue into the 20th century —and indeed in several important ways would characterize it.

MAIN TEXT CONTINUES IN VOLUME 11

William Jennings Bryan

A SPECIAL CONTRIBUTION BY

JOHN A. GARRATY

During his 50 years of public life, Bryan ran for President three times, but at the end he was a relic of the past, an object of ridicule and pity.

"The President of the United States may be an ass," wrote H. L. Mencken during the reign of Calvin Coolidge, "but he at least doesn't believe that the earth is square . . . and that Jonah swallowed the whale." The vitriolic Mencken was comparing President Coolidge to William Jennings Bryan, one of the dominant figures in the Progressive movement. According to Mencken, Bryan was an utter fraud: "If the fellow was sincere, then so was P. T. Barnum."

It was easy for sophisticates to conclude that Bryan was a fake. His undignified association with real estate promotions, his bigoted religious views, his narrow-minded attitude toward alcoholic beverages, and his unabashed political partisanship did not seem to jibe with his pretensions as a reformer. And his oratorical style, magnificent but more emotional than logical, was disappointing to thinking people. David Houston stated that "One could drive a prairie schooner through any part of his argument and never scrape against a fact."

But these flaws should never be allowed to overshadow Bryan's long years of devoted

In 1900, to Bryan's usual campaign issues—the great trusts and bimetallism—was added the imperialism born of the war with Spain.

service to the cause of reform. He was perfectly attuned to the needs and aspirations of rural America. In the early 1890s he was in the forefront of the fight against high tariffs on manufactured goods. Later in the decade he battled for currency reform. At the turn of the century he was leading the assault against imperialism. During Theodore Roosevelt's primacy he advocated a federal income tax, the eight-hour day, the control of monopoly and the strict regulation of public utilities, women's suffrage, and a large number of other startling innovations. Under Wilson he marshaled support in Congress for the Federal Reserve Act and other New Freedom measures. Whatever his limitations, few public men of his era acted as consistently "progressive" as Bryan.

For years he led the Democratic Party without holding office. Three times he was a Presidential candidate; although never elected, he commanded the loyalty of millions. He was more a man of heart than of brain, but his heart was great.

Bryan, aptly known as the Great Commoner, was a man of the people in origin and by instinct. He was born in Salem, Illinois, in 1860, a child of the great Middle West, and he absorbed its spirit and its sense of protest. After being graduated from Illinois College in 1881, he studied law in Chicago. In 1887, he moved west to Lincoln, Nebraska, where he was active in the local Democratic organization, and in 1890, at the age of 30, he won his party's nomination for Congressman.

Nebraska was traditionally a Republican state. But by 1890 tradition was rapidly

891

THIS IS THE BEST COUNTRY ON EARTH!
OURS IS THE BEST GOVERNMENT THE SUN EVER SHONE UPON!
THE ONLY FREE GOVERNMENT UNDER WHICH THE PEOPLE RULE!
AND OUR PEOPLE ARE CAPABLE OF RULING!
THEY DO NOT NEED THE LESSONS OF HISTORY!
THEY HAVE NOTHING TO LEARN!
THEY DO NOT CARE FOR THE EXPERIENCE OF OTHER NATIONS!
THEY KNOW IT ALL!
THEY ARE ALL STATESMEN AND CAN SOLVE THEIR OWN PROBLEMS WITHOUT THE AID OR CONSENT OF ANY OTHER NATION ON EARTH!
STUDY AND SCIENCE ARE OF NO ACCOUNT.
THE POPULAR INTUITION IS BETTER THAN REASONING AND WHAT THE PEOPLE SAY GOES!

16 TO 1

THE DAILY WIND GAUGE

PRESS

losing its hold on voters all over the Middle West. Within a single generation the United States was transformed from a land of farmers into a modern industrial society, and in the process the Middle West was caught in a relentless economic vise. Farmers, who had gone into debt during the Civil War to buy more land and machinery, watched helplessly as the prices of such staple crops as wheat plummeted from $2.50 to 50¢ a bushel. At the same time, the social status of the farmer was declining. Where once he had been a symbol of American self-reliance and civic virtue, now he was often portrayed as a hayseed—a comic mixture of shrewd self-interest and monumental provincialism. Naturally, the farmers resented their loss of both income and prestige, but there was little they could do about either.

Furthermore, the citizens of Nebraska and other agricultural states were convinced that a tiny group of powerful tycoons in great Eastern centers like Boston, New York, and Philadelphia were out to enslave the rest of the country. Useless middlemen grew fat off the mere "handling" of wheat and cotton. Monopolistic railroads overcharged for carrying crops to market; unscrupulous operators of grain elevators charged exorbitant fees. Cynical speculators drove the price of

To the Eastern Republican, Bryan's appeal in 1896 was to a rabble of yokels, and his free coinage of silver at a ratio of 16 to 1 with gold meant the utter ruination of the country.

At first, discontented elements concentrated on opposing the government's policy of retiring the greenbacks. To save this money, a Greenback (later Greenback-Labor) Party sprang up. Meanwhile, the Grange (originally a secret mutual-benefit association of farmers) began to agitate against the middlemen who were draining off the farmers' profits. Although the Grange abandoned political activity in the 1880s, other farm organizations quickly took its place, and around 1890 they united to form the Populist Party.

William Jennings Bryan was a Democrat, but the aspirations and the general point of view of these Midwestern farmers were his own. The farmers themselves were on the lookout for men who understood their problems. In 1888, the Republicans had carried Bryan's Congressional district by 3,000 votes; now, in 1890, the Democrat swept in with a lead of 6,713.

Bryan made an excellent record in his first term. Realizing that the money question was the crucial issue of the day, he was soon deep in a study of it, hoping to find a way to check the deflationary trend that was so injurious to his farmer constituents. He discovered that most farm-belt financial authorities thought this could best be done by providing for the free coinage of silver.

Within a month, Bryan was calling for free coinage, and he stressed the issue in his successful campaign for re-election in 1892. But the new President, Democrat Grover Cleveland, was an ardent gold-standard man, and when a severe depression struck the country early in 1893, he committed his party to the single gold standard.

Bryan, refusing to go along with this policy, threatened to "serve my country and my God under some other name" than Democrat unless the administration changed its mind.

staples up and down, without the slightest regard for the producers whose sweat made their deadly game possible.

Conspiring with bankers and mortgage holders, all these groups combined to dictate the federal government's money policy. Population and production were surging forward; more money was needed. Yet the government was deliberately cutting down on the amount of money in circulation by retiring Civil War greenbacks. On debt-ridden farmers the effect of this deflation was catastrophic.

As neither of the major parties espoused the farmers' cause wholeheartedly, the protest found its way into third-party organizations.

Although Cleveland carried the day for gold, Bryan emerged as a potential leader of the silver wing of the Democrats.

In 1894, he ran for the Senate. In those days Senators were still chosen by the state legislatures. To be elected, Bryan needed the support of Nebraska's Populists as well as that of his own party. He worked hard for fusion, but he did not get Populist support and the Republican candidate won.

Losing did not harm Bryan politically. He was still in his early 30s; to one so young, merely having run for the Senate brought considerable prestige. Also, he had conducted an intelligent and forceful campaign. Even so, it was a defeat, not calculated to lead to the remarkable decision he made— to seek nomination for the Presidency of the United States!

With Cleveland and the national organization dead set against free coinage, Bryan's chances of getting the nomination seemed infinitesimal. But if bold, his action was by no means foolish. Democratic voters were restive under Cleveland's conservative leadership. At least in Bryan's part of the nation, many Democrats were beginning to feel that they must find new leaders if they were not to be replaced by the Populists as the country's second major party. Recognizing this, Bryan proceeded to act with determination and dispatch.

He set out to make himself known beyond his own locality. Accepting the editorship of the *Omaha World-Herald,* he turned out a stream of editorials on the silver question, which he sent to influential politicians all over the country. He toured the South and West, speaking to close-packed, cheering throngs and to tiny groups of quiet listeners. His argument was simple but forceful, his oratory magnetic and compelling. Always he made sure to meet local leaders and to subject them to his genial smile, his youthful vigor, his charm, his sincerity. When the Democratic convention finally met in Chicago, Bryan believed he was known personally to more of the delegates than any other candidate.

Few delegates took his campaign seriously, but the candidate, amiable and serene, took no offense. A majority of the delegates favored his position on silver; no one had a clear lead in the race. All Bryan needed was a chance to plead his case. The opportunity came when he was asked to close the debate on the platform's silver plank. As he came forward to address the jam-packed crowd in the Chicago auditorium, he was tense, but there was a smile on his face. He began quietly, but his voice resounded in the great hall and commanded the attention of every delegate. When he recounted the recent history of the struggle between the forces of gold and silver, the audience responded eagerly. He spoke for silver as against gold, for the West over the East, for "the hardy pioneers who have braved all the dangers of the wilderness" as against "the few financial magnates who, in a back room, corner the money of the world". He continued, "We have petitioned, and our petitions have been scorned; we have entreated, and our entreaties have been disregarded; we have begged, and they have mocked when our calamity came. We beg no longer; we entreat no more; we petition no more. We defy them!"

The crowd thundered its agreement. "Burn down your cities and leave our farms," he said, "and your cities will spring up again as if by magic; but destroy our farms and the grass will grow in the streets of every city in the country." The crowd cheered because he was reflecting its sentiments, but also because it recognized, suddenly, its leader—handsome, confident, righteously indignant, yet also calm, restrained, and ready for responsibility.

Bryan had saved a marvelous figure of speech for his climax: "We will answer their demand for a gold standard by saying to them, 'You shall not press down upon the brow of labor this crown of thorns, you shall not crucify mankind upon a cross of gold.'" Dramatically he extended his arms to the side, the very figure of the crucified Christ.

Amid the hysterical demonstration that followed, it was clear that Bryan had accom-

In 1896, in a speech at Petersburg, Virginia, Bryan claimed no man should leave his party when it is in trouble. The cartoonist points out that this is just what Bryan did in 1892.

POPULIST NOMINATION '92 FOR PRESIDENT

REGULAR DEMOCRATIC NOMINATION '92

J.B. WEAVER

GROVER CLEVELAND

FOR PRESIDENT J.B. WEAVER

BALLOT BOX.

POPULIST PLATFORM '92

FREE COINAGE OF SILVER AT HALF ITS COMMERCIAL VALUE, UNLIMIT-ED PAPER MONEY FOR EVERY BODY, THE CONFISCATION OF ALL RAIL-ROAD, TELEGRAPH AND TELEPHONE LINES — IN SHORT, TRAILING NATIONAL HONOR IN THE MUD OF REPUDIATION

DEMOCRATIC PLATFORM '92

BIMETALLISM THROUGH INTERNATIONAL AGREEMENT OR BY SUCH SAFE GUARDS OF LEGISLATION AS WOULD ENSURE THE PARITY OF BOTH GOLD AND SILVER AND PRESERVE THE NAT-IONAL HONOR.

Keppler.

HE DID NOT THINK SO IN '92.

plished his miracle. The next day, July 9, he was nominated for the Presidency on the fifth ballot.

The issue was clear-cut, for the Republicans had already declared for the gold standard and nominated thoroughly conservative William McKinley. As a result, the Populists were under great pressure to go along with Bryan. To insist on nominating a third candidate would simply insure the election of the "gold bug" McKinley. Not every important Populist favored fusion, but the rich scent of victory was in the air, and the Populist convention endorsed Bryan, too. Thus the silver forces united to do battle with the Republicans.

It was to be a close and crucial election. Seldom have the two great parties divided so clearly on fundamental issues. Silver against gold was but the surface manifestation of the struggle. City against countryside, industry against agriculture, East against South and West, the 19th century against the 20th—these were the real contestants in 1896.

After Bryan's nomination, McKinley's manager, Mark Hanna, raised huge sums by "assessing" the great bankers, oil refiners, insurance men, and meat packers, using the threat of impending business chaos and wild inflation to loosen the purse strings of the tycoons. While McKinley conducted a dignified campaign from his front porch in Canton, Ohio, 1,400 paid speakers beat the bushes for votes. The Republican campaign committee distributed more than 120,000,000 pieces of literature in 10 languages. Hanna, Theodore Roosevelt said, "has advertised McKinley as if he were a patent medicine!"

Bryan had little money and no organizational genius like Hanna to direct his drive. But between summer and November he traveled a precedent-shattering 18,000 miles, making more than 600 speeches and addressing directly an estimated 5,000,000 Americans. His secretary calculated that he spoke between 60,000 and 100,000 words every day during the campaign.

On the stump he was superb. He could make himself heard to a restless open-air throng numbered in the tens of thousands, and he was equally effective from the rear platform of a train speaking to a handful of country people. Thousands of well-wishers sent him good-luck charms and messages of encouragement. "If the people who have given me rabbits' feet in this campaign will vote for me, there is no possible doubt of my election," he said.

Such a campaign is an effective means of projecting an image and a point of view. It is not well suited for the making of complicated arguments and finely drawn distinctions. Wisely, Bryan hammered repeatedly at the currency question. He did not avoid talking about other matters: He attacked the railroads and the "tyranny" of the Eastern bankers. He deplored the use of the militia in labor disputes and the use of the injunction as a means of breaking strikes. He spoke in favor of income taxes, higher wages, and relief for hard-pressed mortgagees. But the silver issue was symbolic, the Democratic position sound, and Bryan emphasized it.

For a time his gallant, singlehanded battle seemed to be having an effect on public opinion, and Republican leaders became thoroughly frightened. Threats and imprecations now became weapons in the campaign. A rumor was circulated that Bryan was insane, and the *New York Times* devoted columns to the possibility. "Men," one manufacturer told his workers, "vote as you please, but if Bryan is elected . . . the whistle will not blow Wednesday morning." A Chicago company that held thousands of farm mortgages politely asked all its "customers" to indicate their Presidential preferences—a not very subtle form of coercion.

By election day, the McKinley managers were confident of victory, but they still put on a final monumental drive to get out the vote. Everywhere in the crucial North Central states the Hanna machine expended enormous efforts. McKinley carried all those states, and with them the nation. In the electoral college, he won by 271 to 176, but the popular vote was close—7,035,638 to 6,467,946.

The victory, however, was McKinley's, and a dividing point in the economic and social history of the United States had been crossed.

The two famous figures of the 1925 Scopes trial are shown during a recess: Clarence Darrow (left), who defended Scopes, and Bryan (right), who spoke for the prosecution.

The rural America of the 19th century was making way for the industrial America of the 20th. Soon business conditions began to improve, agricultural prices inched upward, and new discoveries of gold relieved the pressure on the money supply.

William Jennings Bryan, unchastened by defeat and always cheerful, maintained the leadership of his party. Consistently he took the liberal position on important issues. Running for President a second time in 1900, he made resistance to imperialism an issue in the campaign along with free silver. If both of these positions were poorly calculated to win votes in 1900, they were nonetheless solidly in the liberal tradition. Bryan lost to McKinley again, this time by 861,459 votes. But he continued to fight. In 1904, battling against conservatives in his own party, he forced the adoption of a fairly liberal platform (including strong antitrust, prolabor,

and antitariff planks), and when the conservative Judge Alton B. Parker was nonetheless nominated for President, Bryan kept up his outspoken criticism.

In the campaign of 1908, Bryan, once more the Democratic nominee, was defeated by William Howard Taft. Immediately he announced he would not seek the office again.

Although he thus abandoned formal leadership of the Democrats, Bryan continued to advocate reform. Throughout the Taft administration he campaigned to bolster the liberal wing of his party. When the 1912 nominating convention met in Baltimore, he threw his support to Woodrow Wilson.

Nothing reveals Bryan's fine personal qualities better than his support of Wilson, for the former Princeton professor had opposed the Great Commoner since 1896, when he had called the *Cross of Gold* speech "ridiculous."

In 1908, Wilson had refused to appear on the same platform with him. "Mr. Bryan," he said, "is the most charming and lovable of men personally, but foolish and dangerous in his theoretical beliefs." By 1912, Wilson had become far more liberal and no longer opposed most of Bryan's policies; even so, a lesser man might not have forgiven the repeated criticisms. But Bryan was more concerned with Wilson's 1912 liberalism than with personal matters, and when Wilson paid him a handsome public tribute, they became good friends. Bryan campaigned vigorously for Wilson, making well over 400 speeches within seven weeks. When Wilson won an easy victory, Bryan reacted without a trace of envy or bitterness. "It is a great triumph," he declared. "Let every Democratic heart rejoice."

Wilson made Bryan Secretary of State. He was needed in the administration to help manage his many friends in Congress. The strategy worked well; Bryan used his influence effectively. But in managing foreign affairs he was less successful, for he was ill-prepared. Because of his frank-belief in the spoils system, he dismissed dozens of key professional diplomats, replacing them with untrained political hacks. His policy of not serving alcoholic beverages at official functions because of his personal convictions caused much criticism at home and abroad. "W. J. Bryan not only suffers for his principles and mortifies his flesh, as he has every right to do," the London *Daily Express* complained, "but he insists that others should suffer and be mortified."

Unfortunately, Bryan had but a dim understanding of Latin American problems and unwittingly fostered American imperialism, causing much bad feeling in South and Central America. When World War I started in 1914, Bryan, like his chief, adopted a policy of strict neutrality. He believed in real neutrality far more deeply than Wilson, and when, after the sinking of the *Lusitania,* the President sent threatening messages to Germany, Bryan resigned as Secretary of State. He never again held public office.

It would have been better for Bryan's reputation if he had died in 1915; instead, he lived on for another decade. He made no effort to keep up with the abrupt intellectual developments of the 20th century, yet he was accustomed to speak his mind and continued to do so. More and more he confined himself to religious questions, and though his piety was heartwarming, he was a smug and intolerant Fundamentalist, ignorant of modern science and ethics.

Advancing age made Bryan even less tolerant, and he became, in the 1920s, an outspoken foe of many aspects of human freedom. He defended Prohibition, refused to condemn the Ku Klux Klan, and participated eagerly in the notorious Scopes antievolution trial, with all its overtones of censorship and self-satisfied ignorance.

The final great drama of Bryan's life occurred when Clarence Darrow mercilessly exposed his simple prejudices on the witness stand at that trial. Bryan complacently maintained that Eve was actually made from Adam's rib and that Jonah had really been swallowed by the whale. The rural audience cheered, but educated men all over the world were appalled.

Throughout his lifetime, Bryan was subject to harsh and almost continual criticism. But he was too secure in his faith to be injured by it, and he knew that for over two decades his influence was greater than that of any of his contemporaries except Theodore Roosevelt and Woodrow Wilson. His life was useful and happy, for he rightly believed that he made a lasting contribution to his country's development.

In 1896, he was indeed the peerless leader—vital, dedicated, and, in a measure, imaginative. For years the momentum of 1896 carried him on, but eventually the speeding world left him far behind. He never realized what had happened, and a few days after Darrow had exposed his shallowness before the world, he died peacefully in his sleep, as serene and unruffled by events as ever.

John A. Garraty, chairman of the history department at Columbia University, is the author of many books, including biographies of Henry Cabot Lodge, Sr., and Woodrow Wilson.

Volume 10
ENCYCLOPEDIC SECTION

The two-page reference guide below lists the entries by categories. The entries in this section supplement the subject matter covered in the text of this volume. A **cross-reference** (*see*) means that a separate entry appears elsewhere in this section. However, certain important persons and events mentioned here have individual entries in the Encyclopedic Section of another volume. Consult the Index in Volume 18.

AMERICAN STATESMEN AND POLITICIANS

Nelson W. Aldrich
William B. Allison
John P. Altgeld
Chester A. Arthur
James G. Blaine
Richard P. Bland
Blanche K. Bruce
William Jennings Bryan
Grover Cleveland
Roscoe Conkling

Jacob Coxey
Ignatius Donnelly
James A. Garfield
Benjamin Harrison
Oliver H. Kelley
Mary Elizabeth Lease
George H. Pendleton
Hiram R. Revels
Carl Schurz
Jerry Simpson
James B. Weaver

BUSINESS

Black Friday
Edwin L. Drake
Daniel Drew
James B. Duke
George Eastman
Thomas Alva Edison
James Fisk
Henry Clay Frick
John W. Gates
Jay Gould
Edward H. Harriman
House of Morgan

Ottmar Mergenthaler
J. P. Morgan
Panic of 1873
Panic of 1883
Panic of 1893
George M. Pullman
John D. Rockefeller
Nikola Tesla
Cornelius Vanderbilt
William H. Vanderbilt
George Westinghouse
T. T. Woodruff

INVENTORS

Alexander Graham Bell
George Eastman
Thomas Alva Edison

George M. Pullman
Nikola Tesla
George Westinghouse
T. T. Woodruff

THE LABOR MOVEMENT

American Federation of Labor
Jacob Coxey
Clarence Darrow
Eugene V. Debs
Samuel Gompers

Haymarket Square riot
Homestead strike
Knights of Labor
Henry D. Lloyd
Pullman strike
Uriah S. Stephens

POLITICAL DEVELOPMENTS

American Protective Association
Bland-Allison Act
Chinese Exclusion Act
Credit Mobilier scandal
"Cross of Gold" speech
Dingley Tariff
Federal Immigration Act of 1891
Granges
Greenback Party
Interstate Commerce Act
Liberal Republican Party
McKinley Tariff

Morrill Tariff
Mugwumps
National Farmers' Alliance
New Immigration
Pacific Railway Acts
Patrons of Husbandry
Pendleton Act
People's Party
Plessy vs. Ferguson
Populists
Sherman Antitrust Act
Sherman Silver Purchase Act
Wilson-Gorman Tariff

THE PRESIDENCY

Chester A. Arthur
Grover Cleveland

James A. Garfield
Charles J. Guiteau
Benjamin Harrison

THOUGHT AND CULTURE

Ignatius Donnelly
Wyatt Earp
Ellis Island
Henry George
Edward L. Henry
Jesse James
John Kane

Emma Lazarus
Mary Elizabeth Lease
Henry D. Lloyd
Walter Rauschenbusch
Scopes trial
Statue of Liberty
Coleman Younger

A

ALDRICH, Nelson Wilmarth

ALDRICH, Nelson Wilmarth (1841–1915). As a Republican Senator from his native Rhode Island from 1881 until he retired in 1911, Aldrich dominated his state's politics and was one of the Senate's leading Republicans as well as that party's chief spokesman for the industrial, commercial, and financial interests of the East. A wealthy businessman and a conservative, Aldrich advocated protective tariffs and the gold standard. After entering local politics in 1869, he served in the Rhode Island legislature (1875–1876) and in the House of Representatives (1879–1881) before entering the Senate. He helped eject Republicans who favored the free coinage of silver—a policy advocated by **William Jennings Bryan** (*see*)—from the party. Aldrich supported the Gold Standard Act of 1900 and was influential in securing the passage of the protectionist Payne-Aldrich Tariff of 1909. During his last years in the Senate, Aldrich was mainly concerned with monetary reform. He helped to formulate the Aldrich-Vreeland Act of 1908, which, among other things, established a national monetary commission to study bank reform. Aldrich headed this commission, and in 1911, after an intensive study of banking and currency systems in both the United States and Europe, he published the Aldrich plan of currency legislation. This plan never became law, but the Democratic Party incorporated many of its features into the Federal Reserve System, which was established in 1913. This system reorganized the nation's banking structure.

ALLISON, William Boyd

ALLISON, William Boyd (1829–1908). Allison was an Iowa Republican who served in the United States Senate for 35 years. A native of Ohio, Allison, who was a lawyer, moved to Dubuque, Iowa, in 1833. In the early years of the Civil War, he organized and raised four regiments for the Union Army. In 1862, Allison was elected to the first of four terms (1863–1871) in the House of Representatives, where he established a reputation as a moderate. Ten years later, he entered the United States Senate, to which he was reelected five successive times (1873–1908). For 27 years, Allison was the chairman of the Appropriations Committee and for 30 years a member of the Finance Committee. He favored lower import duties on goods needed by Midwestern farmers, and at the same time he sided with Eastern industrialists who wanted a free rein to expand their transportation and manufacturing interests. He was the coauthor, with **Richard P. Bland** (*see*), of the **Bland-Allison Act** (*see*). This law provided for the government's purchase of silver bullion. Three Presidents—**James A. Garfield, Benjamin Harrison** (*see both*), and William McKinley (1843–1901)—offered Allison posts in their cabinets, but he preferred to remain in the Senate, where he wielded considerable influence and had seniority for committee assignments.

ALTGELD, John Peter

ALTGELD, John Peter (1847–1902). The first Democratic governor (1892–1896) of Illinois since the Civil War, Altgeld was one of the strongest advocates of civil liberties in his day. Brought to Ohio as a baby by his parents, who were German immigrants, Altgeld received little formal schooling. In 1869, he went west, working as a common laborer and teacher and studying law. He moved to Chicago in 1875 and became a lawyer. Altgeld's belief that the poor were treated unfairly under the law led him to publish *Our Penal Machinery and Its Victims* in 1884. Two years later, he was elected a judge on the superior court of Cook County, Illinois, and was chief justice by the time he resigned from the bench in 1891. After successfully running for governor as a Democrat in 1892, Altgeld began implementing his progressive views by improving prisons and charitable institu-

John P. Altgeld

tions and sponsoring child-labor laws. He became the focus of national attention and the butt of criticism in his own state in 1893, when he pardoned the three surviving radical agitators who had been convicted for complicity in inciting the violent **Haymarket Square riot** (*see*). Altgeld believed that their trial had been a miscarriage of justice. He further antagonized his detractors in 1894 when he demanded that President **Grover Cleveland** (*see*) withdraw the federal troops that had been sent to Chicago to quell the **Pullman strike** (*see*). As a result of these controversies, conservative Illinois Republicans labeled Altgeld a radical and successfully ran their own candidate against him when he sought reelection in 1896. Outside Illinois, however, Altgeld won nationwide popularity. Some historians contend that if he had been a native-born citizen, as required by the Constitution, Altgeld and not **William Jennings Bryan** (*see*) would have been the Democratic candidate for President in 1896. He continued to crusade for social reforms until his death.

AMERICAN FEDERATION OF LABOR.

The A.F.L. was organized in 1886 to promote independent trade unionism in America. The formation of the union was, in part, a reaction to the **Knights of Labor** (*see*), a centrally controlled industrial union with broad political and social goals that was accused of being socialist. Under the leadership of **Samuel Gompers** (*see*), the A.F.L. limited membership to skilled workers, opposed political activity not directly related to the union, and regarded collective bargaining as its chief function. Individual workers were not members of the A.F.L. but joined their affiliated local or national union. The federation had no power except what was granted to it by member unions in the federation's constitution or at its annual convention. The federation was charged with the responsibility of working toward the common goals of the member unions. Membership in the federation grew steadily. During World War I, when the A.F.L. obtained unprecedented power and became the recognized spokesman for organized labor, membership soared to 4,000,000. The development of mass-production industries resulted in demands by some A.F.L. members for industrial, as well as craft, unions. The industrial unionists broke away from the A.F.L. and formed the Congress of Industrial Organizations in 1938. The A.F.L. and the C.I.O. merged in 1955 to form the largest confederation of craft and industrial unions in the nation.

AMERICAN PROTECTIVE ASSOCIATION.

This association, founded at Clinton, Iowa, in 1887, was a secret, anti-Catholic, anti-immigrant, patriot group. The growing number of Irish Catholics in the cities had given rise to fear among rural Protestants that "Romanism" would soon be a dominant political force in America. In addition, the tight job market associated with the **Panic of 1893** (*see*) increased bitterness against newly arriving European immigrants, who were competitors for employment. Members of the American Protective Association sought to keep Catholics from holding public office and to prevent parochial schools from sharing in public-school funds. They sponsored anti-Catholic lectures and rallies throughout the nation. By the mid-1890s, the association claimed more than 1,000,000 members, chiefly in the Midwest and New England. It had some success in influencing local and state elections, especially in the Midwest, but failed on the national level. The association began to wither toward the turn of the century. Many farmers joined Catholics in supporting the free-silver policies of **William Jennings Bryan** (*see*). In addition, the appointment of a Catholic, Joseph McKenna (1843–1926), as Attorney General in 1897 was a severe setback. By 1911, the association was out of existence.

ARTHUR, Chester Alan

(1830–1886). Arthur, who was elected Vice-President under **James A. Garfield** (*see*) in 1880, became the nation's 21st President on September 19, 1881, when Garfield died as the result of a gunshot wound inflicted by a rejected office seeker. Although Arthur conducted his administration with energy and integrity, Congressional opposition frustrated much of his proposed legislation. Arthur was born in Fairfield, Vermont. After graduation from Union College in Schenectady, New York, in 1848, he practiced law in New York City, where he allied himself with the powerful state

Chester A. Arthur

Republican organization of Senator **Roscoe Conkling** (*see*). An able administrator, Arthur served as quartermaster general of the state of New York during the Civil War. Arthur's political connections led to his being appointed customs collector of the Port of New York in 1871, but a storm of controversy soon broke over his widespread use of the political spoils system. Although it was a common practice to reward loyal party supporters with government jobs, a reform movement at that time attacked Arthur in order to break the power of Conkling's political machine. President Rutherford B. Hayes (1822–1893), although himself a Republican, had Arthur removed from his post in 1878. Arthur, who was subsequently regarded by Republican politicians as a martyr to party loyalty, was awarded the Republican Vice-Presidential nomination in 1880. Suddenly thrust into the White House when Garfield died after only six months in office, Arthur immediately confounded—and alienated—his former supporters by refusing to implement the spoils system or to be a henchman of self-seeking party leaders. Disgruntled Republicans then combined with the Democratic opposition in Congress to stymie much of his program. Nevertheless, Arthur succeeded in finally eliminating fraudulent practices in the Post Office Department, in reforming the federal civil service (see **Pendleton Act**), and in modernizing the navy. After modification of a treaty with China, he agreed to support the **Chinese Exclusion Act** (see) of 1882. Arthur's independent course cost him the Republican nomination in 1884. The strain of being President exhausted Arthur, and upon leaving office he returned to New York City, where he died 20 months later on November 18, 1886.

B

BELL, Alexander Graham (1847–1922). Bell's invention of the telephone transformed not only the field of communications but the pace and quality of modern life as well—from business transactions to personal relations. Born in Edinburgh, Scotland, Bell was the son of Alexander Melville Bell (1819–1905), who was a pioneer in teaching the deaf to speak. From his father, Bell acquired an interest in speech science and the physical properties of sound that pointed him toward his most revolutionary invention. After studying at the Universities of Edinburgh and London, he became engaged in demonstrating his father's Visible Speech system to teachers of the deaf. The family moved to Canada in 1870, and the next year Bell went to Boston, where he later joined the faculty of Boston University as a professor (1873–1877) of vocal physiology. Bell had begun his scientific investigation into the properties of vocal sound in 1865. In America, he began experimenting with the telegraph, seeking to discover a way to transmit human speech electrically. By 1874, he had conceived the principle of the telephone. Two years later, on March 10, Bell spoke the first words transmitted telephonically, informing his laboratory assistant, "Watson, come here; I want you." The telephone was demonstrated successfully that same year before the American Academy of Arts and Sciences and at the Philadelphia Centennial Exposition (see p. 822). Many others now came forward to claim credit for the discovery, but the courts upheld Bell's patent rights. The invention gained rapid acceptance, and the Bell Telephone Company was established in July, 1877. The following year, Bell moved to Washington, D.C., where he set up the Volta Laboratory and continued with his experiments. From his inventive genius issued such discoveries as the photophone (a device for transmitting sound by light rays), various improvements on the phonograph of **Thomas Edison** (see), and an electric probe for locating bullets in the human body. The probe was used unsuccessfully to try to find a bullet near the spine of President **James A. Garfield** (see), who was assassinated in 1881. In the late 1890s, Bell's interest turned to aeronautics, and in 1907 he formed a group that built several early airplanes. Bell founded the magazine *Science* in 1880, and he served as president (1896–1904) of the National Geographic Society. He personally provided financial backing for many important scientific projects. Throughout his life, Bell maintained an active role in educating the deaf.

BLACK FRIDAY. Known as Black Friday, September 24, 1869, was the culminating day of a plot originated by **Jay Gould, James Fisk** (see both), and other financial speculators to corner the supply of gold in the United States. At that time, greenbacks, or paper money, were legal tender, and gold was a speculative commodity traded on the Gold Exchange, situated in the Gold Room of the New York Stock Exchange. However, gold was used by merchants and bankers in international transactions and for certain other purposes. In the spring of 1869, Gould persuaded Abel Rathbone Corbin, a lobbyist who was the brother-in-law of President Ulysses S. Grant (1822–1885), to try to exert pressure on the President to prevent him from selling gold from the United States Treasury. It thus would be easier to corner the gold market, because New York banks had a low supply of gold, there was little in circulation, and it would have required some time to import gold from Europe. On June 15, 1869, Gould and Fisk entertained Grant aboard Fisk's yacht and tried to discover his gold policy. The President was noncommittal, but Fisk and Gould spread the rumor that he

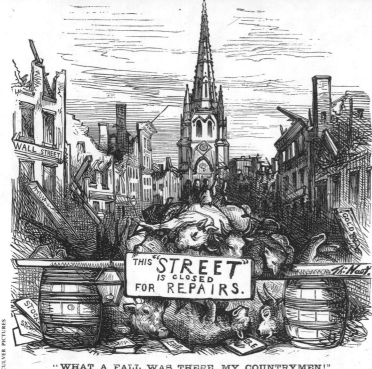

THIS "STREET" IS CLOSED FOR REPAIRS.

GOLD

"WHAT A FALL WAS THERE, MY COUNTRYMEN!"

Thomas Nast viciously depicted the ruin of Wall Street speculators on Black Friday.

was against the sale of government gold. In September, they began buying large quantities of gold, and its price soon rose from 135 to 140, which meant that it required $1.40 in paper money instead of $1.35 to buy one gold dollar. On September 23, the price of gold rose to 144 1/4, and the following day, Black Friday, it soared into the 160s. At this point, Secretary of the Treasury George S. Boutwell (1818–1905) received Grant's permission to sell some of the government's gold, and $4,000,000 worth was immediately put on the market. Within 15 minutes, the price of gold fell to the 130s, and the Gold Exchange closed for the day. Gould and apparently Fisk craftily managed to escape financial embarrassment by selling their holdings upon learning of the government's intention to sell its gold. However, many investors were ruined, and Grant was accused of stupidity for having become involved.

BLAINE, James Gillespie (1830–1893). Although never elected President, Blaine was a constant contender in the years following the Civil War. He was born in Pennsylvania, then moved to Maine, where he became a leader in the state's Republican Party when it was formed in 1854. Blaine was elected to the House of Representatives in 1863. He was chosen Speaker of the House in 1869 and held that position until 1876. Blaine became a leader of the Half Breed Republicans, a faction that opposed the corrupt policies of the Stalwart Republicans. The Stalwarts, who were led by Representative **Roscoe Conkling** (*see*), supported President Ulysses S. Grant (1822–1885). In 1876, Blaine was presented to the Republican National Convention as "a plumed knight," but hurt by charges of corruption while Speaker, he lost the nomination to Rutherford B. Hayes (1822–1893). He then became a Senator (1876–1881) and tried again unsuccessfully to win the Republican nomination for President in 1880. He was defeated by **James A. Garfield** (*see*). Upon

becoming President in 1881, Garfield appointed Blaine his Secretary of State. Blaine resigned after Garfield was assassinated that same year. Finally, in 1884, Blaine won the Republican Presidential nomination. Although he was opposed by reformers in his party who were called **Mugwumps** (*see*), many historians believe that Blaine might have defeated Democrat **Grover Cleveland** (*see*) if one of his supporters had not called the Democrats "the party whose antecedents are rum, Romanism, and rebellion." This charge offended many Irish Catholics in New York. Cleveland won a narrow victory in that state, costing Blaine the election. Four years later, Blaine supported the candidacy of **Benjamin Harrison** (*see*), who subsequently appointed Blaine his Secretary of State (1889–1892) when he became President. Blaine proved a strong leader in foreign affairs. He urged cooperation with the Latin-American nations and created the Pan-American Union in 1889. In 1892, Blaine made his last attempt to become President, but he was defeated by Harrison, who was renominated by the Republican Party.

BLAND, Richard Parks (1835–1899). "Silver Dick" Bland was the leader of the free-silver movement in the House of Representatives in the last quarter of the 19th century. Born in Kentucky, Bland had traveled west in 1855. For 10 years, he worked as a miner and occasional teacher in California, Nevada, and Colorado. The experience left him well acquainted with the problems of silver miners and frontier farmers—the two groups most strongly in favor of free silver. In 1866, Bland settled in Missouri, where he established a law practice. He was elected to Congress six years later. In all, he served 12 terms in the House (1873–1895 and 1897–1899). Bland became chairman of the Committee on Mines and Mining and undertook a campaign to restore silver as a backing for currency. In 1876, he introduced a bill for the free coinage of silver. It was amended in the Senate by **William B. Allison** (*see*) of Iowa and passed, in compromise form, as the **Bland-Allison Act** (*see*) two years later. The act, however, provided for only limited coinage. Thereafter, Bland continued his efforts to secure a free-coinage bill and led the fight in 1893 against the repeal of the **Sherman Silver Purchase Act** (*see*). In 1896, Bland was a candidate for the Democratic Presidential nomination, but he withdrew his name in favor of **William Jennings Bryan** (*see*).

BLAND–ALLISON ACT. The Bland-Allison Act was the first government subsidy to silver producers. The bill, which was introduced in the House of Representatives by **Richard P. Bland** (*see*) of Missouri, provided for the unlimited coinage of silver at the ratio of 16 to 1—that is, 16 ounces of silver were equal in value to one ounce of gold (*see pp. 880–886*). The bill was amended in the Senate, however, by **William B. Allison** (*see*) of Iowa, who substituted limited for unlimited coinage. The act was passed over the veto of President Rutherford B. Hayes

(1822–1893) on February 28, 1878. Under the act, the Secretary of the Treasury was required to purchase, at market prices, not less than $2,000,000 nor more than $4,000,000 worth of silver monthly. The bullion was then to be coined into standard 16-to-1 silver dollars. Because successive Secretaries of the Treasury only purchased the minimum amount monthly, the act had little effect. It was superseded by the passage of the **Sherman Silver Purchase Act** (*see*) in 1890.

BRUCE, Blanche K. (1841–1898). This black statesman was a runaway slave who became a United States Senator and later Register of the Treasury. As Register, his signature was required on all paper currency issued by the federal government. Born in Farmville, Virginia, Bruce ran away from his owner after the Civil War broke out. Able to read and write, he attended Oberlin College in Ohio. After the war was over, he settled in Floreyville, Mississippi, where he became a wealthy planter, taught school, and entered politics. Bruce quickly rose in the ranks of the state's Reconstruction government. In 1874, he was elected as a Republican to the Senate. During his six-year term, Bruce fought for full civil rights for his people and vehemently opposed the abuse of the American Indian and discriminatory legislation

against Chinese immigrants. In a heated debate in the Senate on April 7, 1880, Bruce denounced the government policy "that has kept the Indian a fugitive and a vagabond, that has bred discontent, suspicion, and hatred in the mind of the red man." Because of the overthrow of the Reconstruction regime in Mississippi, Bruce was not reelected to Congress. In 1881, President **James A. Garfield** (*see*) appointed him Register of the Treasury, which meant that all paper currency required a copy of his signature. President **Benjamin Harrison** (*see*) named him Recorder of Deeds for the District of Columbia in 1889, and under President **William McKinley** (1843–1901), Bruce was reappointed Register of the Treasury in 1895, serving in this post until his death.

BRYAN, William Jennings (1860–1925). Bryan was the most powerful figure in the Democratic Party between 1896 and 1912 (*see pp. 890–898*). He won his party's Presidential nomination three times but never attained the White House. Perhaps the most gifted orator of his day, the controversial Bryan was the Great Commoner to millions of hard-pressed farmers, laboring men, and social reformers. To Eastern conservatives, however, he was a windbag and a demagogue, who pitted "the toiling masses" against "Wall Street." A native of Salem, Illinois, Bryan graduated from Illinois College in 1881 and from Chicago's Union College of Law two years later. He was a lawyer at Jacksonville, Illinois, until 1887, when he moved his practice to Lincoln, Nebraska. Bryan gained election to the House of Representatives in 1890, serving until 1895. After losing his bid for a Senate seat in 1894, he became editor of the Omaha, Nebraska, *World-Herald*. Bryan actively

Blanche K. Bruce's signature appears on the lower left of this $2 bill issued in 1896.

sought the Democratic Presidential nomination in 1896. Although only 36 years old and not viewed as a serious contender, he was nominated on the fifth ballot after stampeding the convention with his stirring "Cross of Gold" speech. In it, he attacked the gold standard and demanded the free coinage of silver. The **People's Party** (*see*) also endorsed his candidacy. Despite a determined campaign in which he traveled 18,000 miles through 27 states and delivered more than 600 speeches, Bryan was defeated by the conservative Republican **William McKinley** (*see*) by 600,000 votes. Bryan was again the party standard-bearer in 1900 and was again beaten by McKinley, this time by almost 900,000 votes. In 1901, he founded a weekly newspaper, the *Commoner,* in which he championed "free silver," women's suffrage, and the income tax, and opposed imperialistic territorial expansion by the United States. Judge Alton B. Parker (1852–1926) was the Democratic candidate in 1904, but Bryan recaptured the nomination four years later. He was defeated by William Howard Taft (1857–1930) by more than 1,200,000 votes. Bryan used his influence to help Woodrow Wilson (1856–1924) get the party nomination in 1912 and then served as Secretary of State after Wilson was elected. A consistent advocate of international peace, Bryan negotiated about 30 treaties of arbitration with foreign nations. He resigned in June, 1915, to protest Wilson's increasingly belligerent attitude toward Germany after the sinking of the *Lusitania.* Nevertheless, he supported Wilson's renomination in 1916. Bryan's political influence steadily declined, and as he aged he grew out of touch with the times. An ardent Fundamentalist in religion, he opposed the teaching of evolution and aided the prosecution in the famous **Scopes trial** (*see*) at Dayton, Tennessee, in July, 1925. He died at Dayton on July 26, five days after the trial ended. Bryan's *Memoirs,* completed by his widow after his death, were published in 1925.

C

CHINESE EXCLUSION ACT.

This act, passed in 1882, prohibited the immigration of Chinese laborers to the United States for a period of 10 years. Between 1848 and 1882, about 375,000 Chinese, most of them laborers had entered the nation. This large-scale immigration was encouraged during the 1850s and 1860s, when many unskilled workers were needed to build the nation's growing network of railroads. By the 1870s, however, the large influx of white settlers into the Western states, especially California, had created a condition where there were three men for every job available. The Chinese began to meet with resentment, and then violence. In 1871, agitation against "pig-tailed Orientals" in Los Angeles resulted in a riot that took 21 lives. Similar outbreaks of violence took place in San Francisco and Denver. Ignoring the Burlingame Treaty of 1868, which had guaranteed citizens of China fair treatment and the right to enter America without restriction, Congress first voted to curtail Chinese immigration in 1879. However, President Rutherford B. Hayes (1822–1893) vetoed the measure. Three years later, after the Burlingame Treaty had been modified to allow the President to restrict immigration for a period of time, the Chinese Exclusion Act was enacted with the reluctant support of President **Chester A. Arthur** (*see*). The act was renewed in 1892 and extended indefinitely in 1902. It was repealed in 1943, when 105 Chinese were allowed to enter the United States annually. Meanwhile, the number of Chinese in America had declined from about 107,000 in 1890 to nearly 77,000 in 1940.

CLEVELAND, (Stephen) Grover

(1837–1908). Cleveland—who was the only President to serve two nonconsecutive terms (1885–1889 and 1893–1897) and is therefore designated as the 22nd and the 24th President—was the first Democrat to serve in the White House after the Civil War. Born in New Jersey, Cleveland, who used his middle name as his first name, became a lawyer in 1859. He held several minor political offices in New York State before serving as mayor (1881–1882) of Buffalo and then as governor of the state (1883–1884). His refusal to support Tammany Hall, New York's corrupt Democratic machine, as well as his independence of action as governor, led to his nomination as the "clean-government" Presidential candidate on the Democratic ticket in 1884. The ensuing campaign, in which he ran against the notoriously corrupt **James G. Blaine** (*see*), was one of the dirtiest in American history. Cleveland was elected by a narrow margin with the support of many reform Republicans, known as **Mugwumps** (*see*). A bachelor, Cleveland decided to get married when he was 49 years old. He was the only President ever married in the White House. His marriage to his former ward, Frances Folsom (1864–1947), took place on June 2, 1886, before a wedding party limited to cabinet members. As President, Cleveland pressed for civil-service reforms. During his first administration, about 12,000 jobs ordinarily subject to political appointment were transferred to permanent status. A serious problem of this administration was the surplus revenue that had accumulated in the Treasury, largely because of the high tariffs in effect since the Civil War. This surplus encouraged "pork-barrel" legislation— that is, bills for projects or appropriations enacted as favors for Congressmen who vote with the party in power. Cleveland vetoed many of these projects. He saw the necessity of lowering the tariffs and made that question the main issue of the campaign of 1888. Cleveland lost the election to his Republican opponent, **Benjamin Harrison** (*see*), in a campaign marked by vote frauds in Indiana and bribery in New York City—both on the part of Harrison's followers. However, he defeated Harrison four years later by nearly 400,000 popular votes. Soon after Cleveland assumed office for the second time, the nation was hit by a depression following the **Panic of 1893** (*see*).

Cleveland's inauguration in 1885

The **Sherman Silver Purchase Act** (*see*) of 1890 had helped cause the panic, and in November, 1893, the President succeeded in having the act repealed, thus helping to alleviate the depression. However, the repeal of the act alienated the prosilver faction of the Democratic Party, causing a split in that party's ranks that widened during the next three years. Cleveland still advocated lower tariff rates, but the **Wilson-Gorham Tariff Act** (*see*) of 1894, which reduced some custom duties, did not satisfy him and was enacted without his signature. Cleveland then alienated many workers when he ordered federal troops to Chicago in July, 1894, to put down the **Pullman strike** (*see*) that was paralyzing the nation's railroads. In foreign affairs, Cleveland took a vigorous anti-imperialist stand, notably in March, 1893, when he withdrew a treaty annexing Hawaii to the United States. He also broadened the scope of the Monroe Doctrine in 1895 during the dispute between Britain and Venezuela over the boundary between Venezuela and British Guiana. He insisted that the United States be allowed to arbitrate the matter and persuaded Britain, which had opposed arbitration, to agree to it. In 1897, Cleveland retired to Princeton, New Jersey, where he wrote a series of autobiographical essays that were published in 1904 as *Presidential Problems*. He died at the age of 71 on June 24, 1908.

CONKLING, Roscoe (1829–1888). Conkling, who used federal patronage to build a strong political machine in New York State, was one of the most powerful politicians in America in the last half of the 19th century. In 1858, Conkling was elected to the House of Representatives. He served three terms (1859–1863 and 1865–1867) before being elected a Senator (1867–1881). Following his own theory that "Parties are not built up by deportment, or by ladies' magazines, or gush!" he became the undisputed leader of the Republican Party in New York. During the administration of Rutherford B. Hayes (1822–1893), Conkling's opposition to civil-service reforms led to serious disagreements with the President. At the 1880 Republican National Convention, Conkling led the so-called Stalwart faction of the party, which was against civil-service reforms. It unsuccessfully sought to nominate Ulysses S. Grant (1822–1885) for a third term. Conkling only reluctantly supported **James A. Garfield** (*see*), the party's nominee. Conkling later claimed that Garfield had promised him federal patronage. The President, however, appointed Conkling's bitter personal enemy, **James G. Blaine** (*see*), as Secretary of State. Without consulting Conkling, Garfield then made customhouse appointments in New York. Conkling fought the confirmations and then resigned his Senate seat, convincing his fellow Senator from New York, Thomas C. Platt (1833–1910), to resign with him. Both asked the state legislature to reelect them, but the legislature refused to publicly embarrass the President. Conkling subsequently retired from politics to practice law. In 1882, President **Chester A. Arthur** (*see*), who had once been Conkling's assistant, offered him a Supreme Court appointment, but Conkling declined it because he wanted to continue his profitable legal practice. A strong believer in physical exercise, Conkling, who usually walked several miles from his office to his home in New York City every day, insisted on trying to reach his club during the Blizzard of 1888. It took him three hours to walk the 20 blocks, and he collapsed at the club's entrance. He died of pneumonia and resulting complications shortly afterward.

COXEY, Jacob Sechler (1854–1951). In the depression that followed the **Panic of 1893** (*see*), Coxey led a march of jobless workers to Washington, D.C., to demand an end to unemployment through public-works projects. Coxey, the operator of a successful quarry in Massillon, Ohio, had developed a theory that the issuance of more paper money would cure the nation's economic ills. Aided by a California labor agitator named Carl Browne (1849–1914), Coxey developed the idea of a march on Washington to publicize his theories. He warned that 100,000 of the nation's 3,000,000 jobless would march to demand that the federal government begin a road-building program, backed by $500,000,000 in interest-free bonds. The roads would be built by the unemployed, who would be paid $1.50 a day. The slogan for the march was "Peace on Earth, Good Will to Men, but Death to Interest on Bonds." About 100 marchers, who called themselves The Commonweal of Christ, set forth in wagons, on horses, and on foot from Massillon on Easter Sunday, March 25, 1894, with 43 newspaper reporters following. They were met by large crowds along the way, but few people joined them. However, by mid-April, the marchers had received so much publicity that similar groups were organized and set out from Chicago, Los Angeles, and San Francisco. Many of these protesters hitched rides in railroad boxcars, but few ever reached Washington. By the time that Coxey's followers arrived there on May 1, after a march of about 300 miles, they numbered only about 500. That

The commander of Coxey's army was jailed for walking on the Capitol grass.

day, Coxey rode in a buggy with his wife and infant son, whom he had named Legal Tender. He was arrested for walking on the grass of the Capitol, fined $5, and sentenced to 20 days in jail. With the loss of their "general," Coxey's "army" soon scattered. Coxey returned to Ohio and ran for innumerable public offices, including the Presidency (1932 and 1936) on the Farmer-Labor Party ticket. He was once elected mayor (1931–1933) of Massillon. Coxey led another march on Washington in 1914, again to promote public works, but it failed to generate any enthusiasm or many followers. That same year, he published an autobiography, *Coxey's Own Story*. He lived to be 97, and before his death in Massillon on May 18, 1951, he saw some of his ideas enacted into law during the three administrations (1933–1945) of President Franklin D. Roosevelt (1882–1945).

CREDIT MOBILIER SCANDAL. The corrupt profiteering by high government officials in the building of the first transcontinental railroad became known as the Credit Mobilier scandal. In 1867, a group of businessmen and politicians, who were stockholders in the Union Pacific Railroad, organized a construction company to build the railroad westward from the Missouri River. Appropriating part of the name of a famous French railroad and banking corporation, they called the enterprise Credit Mobilier of America. (*Crédit Mobilier* is French for "Real-Estate Bank.") Through a series of federal loans and land grants (20,000,000 acres), illegal stock and bond sales, and other manipulations, the schemers, led by Representative Oakes Ames (1804–1873) of Massachusetts, collected nearly $20,000,000 more than what was needed to build the railroad. They secretly pocketed the surplus. Fearing an investigation, Ames sold railroad shares to a number of Congressmen, judges, and other prominent officials at par value and let them pay for the stocks out of dividends. During the Presidential campaign of 1872, the New York *Sun* exposed the embezzlement. Ames and Representative James Brooks (1810–1873) of New York were censured by the House, James W. Patterson (1823–1893) of New Hampshire was threatened with expulsion from the Senate, and Vice-President Schuyler Colfax (1823–1885) was politically ruined. Among numerous other politicians tainted by the scandal was **James A. Garfield** (*see*). However, no one was ever indicted for the theft, and the $20,000,000 was never recovered. The Credit Mobilier scandal, one of many episodes of corruption during the administration of Ulysses S. Grant (1822–1885), was one of the factors that caused the **Panic of 1873** (*see*).

"CROSS OF GOLD" SPEECH. *See* **Bryan, William Jennings.**

D

DARROW, Clarence Seward (1857–1938). Darrow ranks as one of the most distinguished—and controversial—attorneys in American legal history. His long and varied career embraced both corporation and labor law, but he is best remembered as a criminal lawyer and a pioneer in the introduction of psychiatric evidence into the courtroom. He defended more than 50 persons charged with murder, only one of whom was executed. Few men of his day intrigued the public as did the complex Darrow. He was both a humanitarian and a cynical realist. He crusaded for civil rights for blacks but ignored women's suffrage. His life and ideas in part echoed and in part altered the America of the early 20th century. A native of Kinsman, Ohio, Darrow was admitted to the bar in

CULVER PICTURES

Clarence Darrow

1878, after a year of study at Allegheny College in Pennsylvania and a year at the University of Michigan Law School. He practiced in small Ohio towns for nine years before moving to Chicago, where he became a corporation counsel for the city and then an attorney for the Chicago & North Western Railway. In 1894, out of sympathy with the American Railway Union, Darrow resigned his post to defend the union president, **Eugene V. Debs,** following the **Pullman strike** (*see both*). After this case, he became closely identified with the organized-labor movement for the next two decades. In 1907, Darrow won acquittal for William D. "Big Bill" Haywood and the other leaders of the Western Federation of Miners, who had been charged with conspiracy in the murder two years before of former Idaho Governor Frank R. Steunenberg. Four years later, Darrow represented labor leaders James B. and John J. McNamara, who had been indicted in the bombing of the Los Angeles *Times*. After the McNamara brothers confessed to the crime and changed their pleas from not guilty to guilty, Darrow himself was indicted for allegedly trying to bribe a member of the jury. He was finally acquitted after two sensational trials. However, the unfavorable publicity hurt his law practice, and he returned to Chicago to reestablish his reputation. His thorough mastery of the details of the cases he defended and his courtroom skill soon brought him international fame. In 1924, as defense counsel in the sensational Leopold-Loeb murder trial in Chicago, Darrow based his defense on a plea of temporary insanity. As a result, his two clients received life sentences, instead of the electric chair. The following year, Darrow advanced the cause of academic freedom in his brilliant conduct of the **Scopes trial** (*see*), in which he defended a schoolteacher charged with violating a Tennessee law against the teaching of evolutionary theory in public schools. A lifelong opponent of capital punishment as well as a religious skeptic and a social reformer, Darrow set forth his views in eight books, among them *Crime: Its Cause and Treatment* (1925) and *The Story of My Life* (1932).

DEBS, Eugene Victor (1855–1926). This pioneer labor leader unsuccessfully ran five times for President as the Socialist Party candidate. The son of immigrant parents who settled in Terre Haute, Indiana, Debs went to work for a railroad at the age of 15. In 1875, he helped organize the Brotherhood of Locomotive Firemen, and five years later he was elected a national officer. In favor of industry-wide unions, rather than unions limited to a particular craft, Debs resigned from the brotherhood to form the American Railway Union in 1893. The union met with initial success. The Great Northern Railroad acceded to wage demands after an 18-day strike in April, 1894. In June, however, the union ignored a federal court injunction and, in sympathy with the **Pullman strike** (*see*) in Chicago, refused to service Pullman cars. Debs was sentenced to six months in prison for violating the injunction. While in prison, he became a convert to socialism, and in 1897 he transformed the American Railway Union into what later became the Socialist Party of America. Debs was its Presidential nominee in five elections between 1900 and 1920, declining the nomination only in 1916. He received his highest percentage of the popular vote—nearly 6%, or about 900,000 votes—in 1912. Debs' message was a simple one. Socialism, he said, was the remedy for all of the evils inherent in

Eugene V. Debs

a capitalist society. In 1905, Debs helped to found a new labor union, the Industrial Workers of the World, but he subsequently disagreed with the group's more radical policies and withdrew. Debs and the Socialists opposed America's entry into World War I. In 1918, he was sentenced to 10 years in prison for violation of the Espionage Act, which provided severe punishment for anyone making derogatory statements about the government during wartime. Although he was in prison, Debs polled more than 919,000 votes—about 4% of the total vote—in the Presidential election of 1920. President Warren G. Harding (1865–1923) pardoned him in 1921 but did not fully restore his civil rights. Debs then wrote a series of articles on prison conditions, which were published as a book, *Walls and Bars,* a year after his death.

DINGLEY TARIFF. The Dingley Tariff was a protective tariff passed by Congress on July 7, 1897. It was prepared by Representative Nelson Dingley (1832–1899) of Maine, who was the chairman of the House Ways and Means Committee. Tariff rates were raised to an average level of 57%, the highest ever enacted by Congress. Duties on wool and hide were restored, and those on silk and linen were increased. The purpose of the tariff was not revenue. The tariff was primarily intended to protect American industry from foreign competition (*see pp. 858–859*). The Dingley Tariff remained in force until 1909, when it was modified by the Payne-Aldrich Tariff.

DONNELLY, Ignatius (1831–1901). This journalist and politician was active in many of the reform movements of the late 19th century. Born in Philadelphia, Donnelly attended public schools and studied law. About 1857, he moved to Minnesota, where he became a farmer and, running as a Republican, was elected lieutenant governor (1859–1863) of the state. Donnelly began the first of three consecutive terms in the House of Representatives in 1863, during which he supported the Civil War and the Reconstruction policies of his party. However, state Republican leaders denied him a fourth term in 1869 because of his support of land grants to railroads. Donnelly subsequently left the party and joined, successively, the **Liberal Republican Party,** the **Granges,** and the **Greenback Party** (*see all*). He supported their reformist views in an independent weekly journal, *Anti-Monopolist,* which he edited from 1874 to 1879. Eight years later, Donnelly became a leader of the **National Farmers' Alliance** (*see*) and later led its members into the **People's Party** (*see*), which he helped to found. As a Populist, he ran unsuccessfully for governor of Minnesota in 1892 and for Vice-President in 1900. During his lifetime, Donnelly wrote utopian fiction—such as *Atlantis: the Antediluvian World* (1882), a best seller that went through 50 printings—and books dealing with unprovable theories, among them *The Great Cryptogram* (1888), which attempts to show that Francis Bacon (1561–1626) wrote the works of William Shakespeare (1564–1616).

DRAKE, Edwin Laurentine (1819–1880). This pioneer in the petroleum industry was the first man to strike oil at its source and started a nationwide rush for "black gold." Born in Greenville, New York, Drake received a rudimentary education and held various jobs until about 1850, when he became a conductor on the New York and New Haven Railroad. He resigned in 1857 on account of ill health and later that year, as a stockholder in the Pennsylvania Rock Oil Company, was commissioned by the company to visit its land on Oil Creek, near Titusville, Pennsylvania. Until then, only petroleum that rose to the surface of the earth to form pools had been collected and refined. Drake went with a letter of introduction from the company that identified him as "Colonel" Drake, a title the company thought would be impressive. During his brief stay in Titusville, Drake became enthusiastic about the possibilities of drilling into the ground for oil. When he returned, the Pennsylvania Rock Oil Company was dissolved and the Seneca Oil Company was formed. The new company leased Drake its property on the condition that he pay it 12¢ for every barrel of oil produced. With a partner and two former salt-well drillers, Drake immediately began drilling for oil. After 19 months of difficulties, he finally struck oil on August 27, 1859, at a depth of about 69 feet (*see p. 817*). At the outset, 25 barrels were pumped out every day. This later increased to 40 barrels and sold for about $20 a barrel. In addition to proving the existence of oil reservoirs below the earth's surface, Drake also invented a way to prevent the seepage of quicksand or clay into the drill hole, but he failed to patent the idea. His meager profits from the Titusville well were later lost in oil speculation schemes.

DREW, Daniel (1797–1879). A crafty financier, Drew became notorious for his dishonest business practices. A native of upstate New York, Drew served briefly in the War of 1812 and later engaged in horse trading and the cattle business. In 1829, he settled in New York City and soon owned the principal stockyards in the city. Drew entered the steamboat business in 1834 and successfully broke the monopoly held by **Cornelius Vanderbilt** (*see*) on Hudson River traffic. Ten years later, Drew had accumulated enough capital to become a Wall Street broker. Although he could not read or write, he got himself elected to the board of the Erie Railroad in 1857 and manipulated its stock for his own benefit. He was foiled by Vanderbilt in an 1864 attempt to control the railroad lines running into New York City. Drew revenged himself in the bitter stock-market dispute known as the Erie war. Aided by **Jay Gould** and **James Fisk** (*see both*), Drew depressed the price of Erie stock in 1868. The three men made much money themselves but brought ruin to thousands of shareholders and caused Vanderbilt to lose millions of dollars. Drew's fortunes fell after 1870 when his partners turned against him, and he was forced into bankruptcy in 1873. Although he was unscrupulous, Drew, while still rich, endowed

Drew Theological Seminary (now Drew University) in Madison, New Jersey.

DUKE, James Buchanan (1856–1925). This industrialist and philanthropist helped to rebuild the economy of the post-Civil War South by establishing a tobacco industry of unprecedented scope. Born near Durham, North Carolina, Duke began packaging tobacco with his father and brother after the Civil War and by 1874 had founded a tobacco factory at Durham. By using a cigarette-making machine, Duke was able to cut the price of cigarettes, which had previously been produced by a costly manual process. He then distributed them on a nationwide scale. Duke opened a branch factory in New York in 1884, and he soon was manufacturing half the nation's cigarettes, exporting his products overseas, and spending hundreds of thousands of dollars annually on advertising. In 1890, Duke waged the "tobacco war" against his four major competitors that resulted in the companies' merging to form the American Tobacco Company. Duke then absorbed other branches of the tobacco industry into this giant combine and by 1911 controlled 150 factories worth more than $500,000,000. That same year, the Supreme Court ruled that the American Tobacco Company was a monopoly in restraint of trade and ordered its dissolution. Although the company still exists, it only manufactures its own brands and has expanded into other fields. During his lifetime, Duke also pioneered the development of waterpower in the southern Piedmont area, which by 1924 was supplying electricity to cotton mills, factories, and cities. He also established the Duke Endowment, a trust fund that dispensed

much of his fortune to stipulated beneficiaries. Trinity College at Durham was renamed Duke University in his honor in 1924.

E

EARP, Wyatt Berry Stapp (1848–1929). Reputedly "the fastest gun in the West," Earp—contrary to the legend that grew up about his defense of law and order—was a notorious gunfighter. He drifted from Arkansas to Wichita, Kansas, then a rowdy frontier town, in 1874. He became a policeman there the following year but was arrested for violating the peace and dismissed from the force in 1876. Earp then moved to Dodge City, where he served as assistant marshal (1876 and 1878–1879) and also was a card dealer at a local

Wyatt Earp

saloon frequented by his friend, Bat Masterson (1853–1921). In 1879, Earp moved to Tombstone, Arizona, where he worked as a shotgun messenger for Wells, Fargo & Company. He again dealt cards at a local saloon and served briefly as deputy sheriff of Pima County. He and an alcoholic dentist, Doc Holliday, were accused of holding up a stagecoach in March, 1881, and killing the driver and one passenger. Earp allegedly tried to bribe a cattle rustler named Ike Clanton to frame his accomplices in another holdup. When Clanton refused, Earp, along with his two brothers—Morgan and Virgil—and Doc Holliday, trapped Clanton and four other men in a celebrated gunfight at the O. K. Corral on October 26, 1881. Three of Clanton's companions were killed in the encounter. The citizens of Tombstone took it upon themselves to revenge the slayings. Virgil was wounded in an ambush that December, and Morgan was killed in March, 1862, by a sniper. Earp, who had been deputized a federal marshal, then rode out of Tombstone to find Morgan's killer. He never returned, riding instead to the safety of Denver. There, he again found work, at a faro palace called the Central. Toward the end of his life, Earp dabbled in confidence games but lived principally off his investments.

EASTMAN, George (1854–1932). A pioneer in photography, Eastman invented flexible film in 1884 and four years later began manufacturing a small box camera, which he named the Kodak after the sound (ko-dak) that its shutter made when it opened and closed. These two inventions revolutionized the photographic industry. Prior to the invention of flexible film, one of the standard types of negative was a glass plate that had to be coated by hand with a gelatin mixture. Such plates were then inserted into a camera, one at a time, to be exposed. Eastman, who was born in upstate New York, had worked in an insurance office and then in a bank before he patented in 1879 a

Film inventor Eastman watches Edison crank a movie camera in 1928.

process to coat the plates by machine. The following year, he began manufacturing these machine-coated plates at a factory in Rochester, New York. Five years after he invented flexible, paper-backed film in 1884, one of Eastman's chemists developed a film whose coating was placed on transparent backing instead of on paper. In 1891, **Thomas Edison** (*see*) used this new film in his kinetoscope, the forerunner of the movie camera. The Eastman Kodak Company, officially formed in 1892, began selling pocket Kodaks in 1895 and folding cameras in 1897. It subsequently expanded its operations and by the turn of the century was the world's largest photographic-supply manufacturer. A commercially practical color film was developed in 1928. Eastman amassed a vast fortune. He introduced a profit-sharing plan for his employees and contributed generously to, among others, the University of Rochester and the Eastman School of Music, both in Rochester, the Massachusetts Institute of Technology, the Tuskegee Institute in Alabama, the Hampton Institute in Virginia, and the Rochester Dental Dispensary. Eastman, who had no family, committed suicide in 1932, leaving a note that said,

"My work is done, why wait?" Today, the Eastman Kodak Company, which has subsidiaries all over the world, still makes cameras and film but also manufactures chemicals and electronic equipment.

EDISON, Thomas Alva (1847–1931). The man who said, "Genius is two percent inspiration and ninety-eight percent perspiration" was one of the most ingenious inventors in American history. Edison held more than 1,000 patents and is best remembered for inventing the phonograph (*see p. 833*) in 1877 and devising the first commercially successful electric light bulb two years later. Although Edison did not invent the light bulb, he developed a durable filament that made its use practical. Born in Ohio, Edison had only three months of formal schooling. He worked as a newsboy and then as a telegraph operator before patenting his first invention, an electrical vote recorder, in 1869. When he could not find a buyer for it, he decided to devote himself to the invention of products in "commercial demand." Edison moved to New York that year and became a partner in an electrical-engineering company. The sale of this firm in 1870 brought him $40,000, which he used to set up his own electrical-manufacturing shop in Newark, New Jersey. He then hired skilled assistants to collaborate with him on his inventions. For the next five years, Edison concentrated on devising ways to improve the telegraph. One of his most important inventions in this field was an improved stock-market ticker, which was used on the New York Stock Exchange until the 1930s. He also significantly improved the typewriter. In 1876, Edison established his famous "invention laboratory" at Menlo Park, New Jersey. It was the prototype of the modern industrial research laboratory and was staffed with a group of experts who, working under Edison's direction, tested, improved, and invented commercially profitable products. It was there that "the wizard of Menlo Park" constructed the phonograph—which is considered his only completely original invention—and improved the light bulb. Edison then developed a complete electrical system for the distribution of light and power. This research culminated in his greatest technological achievement, the opening in 1882 of the world's first central electric-light power plant. This plant, which was situated on Pearl Street in New York City, was the beginning of the electrical-power industry in America. Edison also organized companies to manufacture light bulbs and the various parts of his lighting system. A merger of these companies in 1889 led to the formation of the Edison General Electric Company, which later became the General Electric Company, now one of the world's largest industrial manufacturing concerns. In 1887, Edison moved his laboratory to larger and more modern facilities in West Orange, New Jersey. Among his numerous

other inventions and improvements, some of the best-known are the storage battery, the dictaphone, the mimeograph, the electric dynamo, the electric locomotive, and the fluoroscope. Edison was also a pioneer in the motion-picture industry. In 1889, one of his research assistants produced a motion-picture camera, called the kinetograph, and a single-viewing projector, called the kinetoscope. The pictures were taken with a transparent film developed under the direction of **George Eastman** (*see*). Edison later developed a large wall projector named the Vitascope and synchronized motion pictures with sound, thereby laying the foundation for talking movies.

ELLIS ISLAND. Ellis Island was the "gateway to the Promised Land" for more than 20,000,000 European immigrants who came to settle in America. The 27-acre

island, situated in upper New York Bay, was the major United States immigration station from 1892 until 1954. The island was named for Samuel Ellis, a butcher, who owned it in 1785. In 1808, the federal government acquired the property. A fort and later a powder arsenal were built on the site. In 1892, Ellis Island became the principal immigration center in America. Its buildings included hospital rooms, recreation rooms, dormitories, and guardhouses. As many as 1,000 people were employed there as doctors, nurses, interpreters, inspectors, guards, and cooks to process the nearly 5,000 immigrants who came through daily. Most of the immigrants came as steerage passengers on the great ocean liners. While he was on board ship, a paper with the immigrant's name, age, occupation, and other data was pinned to his clothing. On Ellis Island, this information was used to

CULVER PICTURES

Immigrant women and children eat their first meal in America on Ellis Island.

make up groups of about 30 persons of similar background, who were then processed together in assembly-line fashion. Doctors checked for contagious diseases, and tests were given to exclude the insane or disturbed. Interrogators sought to weed out anarchists and possible welfare cases. After 1924, the flow of immigration was cut down by restrictive laws, and in 1943 the island was turned into a detention station for deportees or aliens. Eleven years later, the remaining immigration facilities were closed. Ellis Island is now part of the Statue of Liberty National Monument. Since the restoration of the Statue of Liberty, plans have been developed for Ellis Island as a museum and conference center.

F

FEDERAL IMMIGRATION ACT OF 1891.

With an ever-increasing number of aliens arriving in the United States during the so-called **New Immigration** (*see*), Congress passed this first comprehensive immigration law. It was a restrictive act that enlarged the categories of aliens excluded in an act passed in 1882, which banned the entry of criminals, the insane, paupers, and other undesirables. Chinese were already excluded under the **Chinese Exclusion Act** (*see*) passed that same year. In addition to those already excluded, the new act prohibited the immigration of "idiots," "persons likely to become a public charge," and "persons suffering from a loathsome or a dangerous contagious disease." Felons and polygamists were also denied entry. A $1,000 fine or one year's imprisonment, or both, were declared the penalty for anyone convicted of bringing in an alien not entitled to lawful entry. In addition, the act put immigration under the full supervision of the federal government. The office of superintendent of immigration was created within the Treasury Department, and its holder was to be appointed by the President. The act also signaled the beginning of careful examination of immigrants at ports of entry such as **Ellis Island** (*see*). It provided that all aliens were to be given medical examinations by doctors of the Marine Hospital Service. If an alien was found ineligible, the owner of the ship he arrived on had to pay the cost of the immigrant's return trip as well as his living expenses while awaiting transportation. Failure to do so would result in a $300 fine and denial of port clearance until its payment. The Act of 1891 was amended in 1903 to exclude epileptics, prostitutes, and anarchists. The new law also fined shipowners who brought over persons with obvious loathsome or dangerous diseases. This led to an examination of proposed immigrants at the point of departure by the shipping companies.

FISK, James (1834-1872).

A flashy and unscrupulous stock-market speculator, "Jubilee Jim" Fisk reaped a fortune from his shady business dealings, which proved nearly ruinous to the nation's economy (*see pp. 864-865*). Born in Bennington, Vermont, Fisk was an energetic and enterprising man who became wealthy during the Civil War by buying cotton from Union-occupied sections of the South and selling it in the North. He also sold Confederate bonds to British investors. Fisk established a dry-goods business in Boston, but he lost it in the postwar depression. He then moved to New York City, where he founded a brokerage house. In 1868, Fisk, along with **Jay Gould** and **Daniel Drew** (*see both*), waged the "Erie war" to foil the attempt of **Cornelius Vanderbilt** (*see*) to gain control of the Erie Railroad. The three men netted huge profits, but in so doing they nearly wrecked the railroad and came to be regarded as public enemies. In 1868-1869, the partners tried to raise the price of gold and tighten credit, which resulted in **Black Friday** (*see*), the crisis that caused many Americans to lose their investments. Fisk later speculated in steamboats and theatrical productions. He was fatally shot on January 6, 1872, by a rival for the affections of an actress.

FRICK, Henry Clay (1849-1919).

This Pennsylvania-born financier was one of America's greatest leaders in the coke and steel industries. In 1877, at the age of 22, Frick founded Frick & Company, which operated coke ovens in the coalfields of Pennsylvania. During the **Panic of 1873** (*see*), he bought

Henry Clay Frick

out competitors, and by the time he was 30 he was the millionaire "coke king" of America. In the early 1880s, Andrew Carnegie (1835-1919) bought stock in Frick's company because coke was vital to his steel operations. Impressed by Frick's business ability, Carnegie asked him to be the chairman of his steel company in 1889. Frick subsequently played a crucial role in reorganizing it into the Carnegie Steel Company in 1892. He then bought out its chief competitor, the Duquesne Steel Company, built connecting railroads, introduced improved operating techniques, and purchased valuable iron-ore lands in the region around Lake Superior. During the infamous **Homestead strike** (*see*) of 1892 at the Carnegie steel plant in Homestead, Pennsylvania, Frick employed 300 Pinkerton guards to protect the plant from the striking workers. The Pinkerton men and strikers fought an armed battle in which several men were killed and wounded. Shortly after the strike was broken, Frick was shot and stabbed in an assassination attempt by a Russian anarchist, Alexander Berkman (1870-1936). In 1899, after a fight for control of the Carnegie Steel Company, Frick and Carnegie split up. Two years later, Frick helped **J. P. Morgan** (*see*) to organize the United States Steel Corporation, which then bought out the Carnegie company. Frick later became the director of several railroads, notably the Pennsylvania, and in 1919 financed a propaganda campaign aimed at preventing the United States from joining the League of Nations. Frick's mansion off Fifth Avenue in New York City, which contains his valuable collection of old masters, was willed to the city and opened to the public as the Frick Museum in 1935.

G

GARFIELD, James Abram (1831-1881). The 20th President of the United States, Garfield died after only six and a half months in office from a wound inflicted by an assassin. Garfield was born in a log cabin on a farm in Ohio. At the age of 18, he joined the Disciples of Christ and for a while considered becoming a minister. However, he decided to go to Williams College, Williamstown, Massachusetts, and completed his studies there. He returned after graduating in 1856 and became a teacher at the Western Reserve Eclectic Institute (now Hiram College). In 1859, Garfield was elected to the state senate, serving for two years. Garfield helped to organize a regiment at the outbreak of the Civil War and, as a staff officer, rose to the rank of major general. In 1862, he was elected to the House of Representatives and resigned from the army the following year to take his seat. Garfield served nine terms in the House (1863-1880), being reelected despite his rumored involvement in two scandals, one of which was the **Credit Mobilier scandal** (*see*). After the death of Thaddeus Stevens (1792-1868), Garfield and **James G. Blaine** (*see*) became the recognized Republican leaders in the House. When Blaine was elected to the Senate in 1876, Garfield took over as chief spokesman for the Republican Party. The Ohio legislature elected Garfield to the Senate four years later, but he never took his seat. At the Republican National Convention that same year, Garfield managed the nomination campaign of John Sherman (1823-1900), a Senator from Ohio. Ulysses S. Grant (1822-1885) and Blaine opposed Sherman, and the convention was deadlocked. On the 35th ballot, some Sherman delegates bolted to Garfield, and he was nominated unanimously on the next ballot. **Chester A. Arthur** (*see*) was then chosen as his running mate. Garfield's Democratic opponent was General Winfield Scott Hancock (1824-1886). Of the nearly 9,000,000 votes cast, Garfield's plurality was just under 10,000, but he received 214 electoral votes to Hancock's 155. Garfield, who had shown little originality in his Congressional career, did not have enough time to prove his abilities as President. He had indicated that he would not knuckle under to the New York State boss, **Roscoe Conkling** (*see*), by making federal appointments in New York without consulting Conkling. He had also begun prosecuting scandals in the Post Office Department. However, on July 2, 1881, while heading for a train to take him to Williams College where he was to deliver the commencement address, Garfield was shot in the Washington Depot by **Charles J. Guiteau** (*see*), a disappointed office seeker. One of the bullets entered Garfield's back, near the spine. For two and a half months, doctors tried to save his life. The public was never informed of how serious his condition was, and, in fact, the doctors believed he would recover. In August, Garfield, who remained conscious throughout his ordeal, asked to be taken to his seaside summer home in Elberon, New Jersey. He died there on September 19, 1881.

GATES, John Warren (1855-1911). Gates was a businessman and speculator who displayed so much confidence that he was nicknamed Bet A Million. He made his first fortune by developing a market for barbed wire. Finding Texas ranchers skeptical about the merits of his product, Gates in 1878 built a corral of the wire and challenged the ranchers to test its endurance. The wire held, and Gates' career was launched. He subsequently established a manufacturing plant in St. Louis that, through a series of mergers, became the American Steel and Wire Company. It was worth $90,-000,000 in 1898. The previous year, Gates was said to have made $12,000,000 in the stock market. Gates also participated in the formation of the Republic Iron and Steel Company and was part of a syndicate that took over the Tennessee Coal and Iron Company in 1906. Toward the end of his career, Gates lost part of his fortune in Wall Street maneuvers engineered by **J. P. Morgan** (*see*). He moved to Texas, where he entered the oil business. At his death, Gates owned vast real-estate holdings and controlled a number of industries in Port Arthur, Texas.

GEORGE, Henry (1839–1897). An economist and social reformer, George set forth his famous "single tax" theory in *Progress and Poverty,* published in 1879. George maintained that the community, not the individual, was responsible for the value of land. Hence, he said, proceeds from rent and increases in land value should benefit all members of society, not just the owners of property. If this were done, he concluded, a single tax on rent income would be all that was needed to pay all the costs of government. George was born into a poor family in Philadelphia. He went to sea at 16 and then settled in California two years later, working as a printer and journalist in San Francisco, Oakland, and Sacramento. His own hardships and the contrast he saw between great wealth and the poverty it seemed to produce led him to conclude that economic suffering could be eliminated by preventing the few from exploiting the natural resources that rightly belonged to everybody.

His basic ideas were sketched in *Our Land and Land Policy* in 1871 and elaborated upon eight years later in the classic *Progress and Poverty*. After an initial printing of only 500, the book sold several million copies throughout the world. After moving to New York in 1880, George continued to write and lecture widely. Running on a reform platform in the New York mayoral race in 1886, he outpolled the Republican candidate, Theodore Roosevelt (1858–1919), but was defeated by the Democratic nominee, Abram S. Hewitt (1822–1903). George died of an apoplectic stroke 11 years later while again campaigning for mayor of New York. His ideas have influenced various progressive movements and tax legislation in many nations.

GOMPERS, Samuel (1850–1924). Gompers was one of the founders of the **American Federation of Labor** (*see*) and served as the union's president for 37 years.

Samuel Gompers

Born in England, he immigrated to America in 1863 and went to work for his father as an appren-

tice cigar maker. The following year, he joined the local Cigar Makers' Union, and while still in his 20s he was named its president. Under Gompers' leadership, the local became the model for strong unionism in America. The power of national union leaders was strengthened, and membership dues were increased to provide greater benefits to members. In 1881, Gompers was instrumental in organizing a national federation of craft unions, which in 1886 became the American Federation of Labor. As the first president of the A.F.L., Gompers sought higher wages, shorter hours, and better working conditions for union members. Membership grew steadily, and the A.F.L. soon replaced the **Knights of Labor** (*see*) as the most powerful union in the country. Gompers opposed industrial unions—made up of both skilled and unskilled workers—favoring instead craft unions organized along workers' specialties. He also was against the involvement of unions in politics. With the exception of 1895, Gompers was president of the A.F.L. until his death. Just before the outbreak of World War I, President Woodrow Wilson (1856–1924) named him to the Council of National Defense. During the conflict, he organized the War Committee on Labor to support the war effort. At the peace conference at Versailles, France, following the war, Gompers served as chairman of the Commission on International Labor Legislation. His two-volume autobiography, *Seventy Years of Life and Labor,* was published a year after he died.

GOULD, Jay (1836–1892). A ruthless and unscrupulous financier and speculator, Gould rose from humble beginnings to become the owner of half the railroad mileage in the Southwest by 1890 (*see pp. 864–865*). Born in upstate New York, Gould began his career first as a country-store clerk and then as a surveyor. He later operated a tannery and worked as a leather merchant before he began speculating in small railroads. In 1867, he became a director of the Erie Railroad, and with **James Fisk** and **Daniel Drew** (*see both*) he engaged in a spectacular battle to keep **Cornelius Vanderbilt** (*see*) from gaining control of the Erie. Through illegal practices such as stock watering and bribery, the three men managed to oust Vanderbilt the following year. With Fisk as his main partner, Gould next turned to a scheme to corner the gold market, which culminated in a stock-market panic on September 24, 1869, known as **Black Friday** (*see*). Widespread public indignation at his underhanded business methods led to his being forced out of the Erie in 1872. Gould, with a fortune estimated at $25,000,000, then began buying up a vast network of Western railroads, including the Union Pacific. His other business activities included ownership of the New York *World,* virtual ownership of all the elevated railways in New York City, and control of the Western Union Telegraph Company.

GRANGES. Local units—or Granges—of the Patrons of Husbandry flourished during the early 1870s as an instrument of farmers' protests against the economic abuses of the day. Founded in 1867 in Washington, D.C., as a social, fraternal, and educational order by **Oliver Hudson Kelley** (*see*), the Patrons of Husbandry soon had branches in the rural areas of the Midwest. By 1870, there were Granges in nine states, and three years later all but four states of the nation had Granges.

Farmers in grain-growing regions joined the Granges primarily to voice their anger over the monopolistic practices of railroads and grain elevators. The Granges soon became a potent political force, and their agitation resulted in the passage of "Granger laws" in several states. The first such law, enacted by Illinois in 1871, empowered a commission to set maximum rates on freight and passenger trains. The railroads ignored all such legislation until 1877, when the United States Supreme Court upheld the constitutionality of the Granger laws. The Court declared that private property devoted to public use should be subject to state regulation. The Granges also became involved in cooperative business ventures. They established grain elevators, creameries, and general stores. They also tried to manufacture farm machinery, but this proved to be financially disastrous and led to the decline of the Granges after 1876. Many Granges still exist as social associations, mostly in the northeast.

GREENBACK PARTY. The Independent National Party, which was popularly known as the Greenback Party, was organized in 1874 in an effort to put more money into circulation and ease the burden on farmers. Falling agricultural prices, debts incurred during the Civil War, and the **Panic of 1873** (*see*) had combined to bring on hard times for the farmers, especially those in the Midwest and the South. They demanded that the federal government increase the amount of money in circulation by issuing vast quantities of "greenbacks"— legal-tender notes not redeemable in specie (gold or silver). Advocates of this "cheap-money" policy made up the ranks of the Greenback Party. In 1876, the

Grangers tried to "awaken" Americans to the railroads' unfair practices.

party nominated Peter Cooper (1791–1883) of New York for the Presidency, but he received only about 80,000 votes, or less than 1% of the total vote. In order to obtain backing from urban workers, the party was reorganized in 1878 and renamed the Greenback-Labor Party. In the Congressional elections of that year, 14 Greenbackers were sent to the House of Representatives. Two years later, the party nominated Iowa Representative **James B. Weaver** (*see*) for President, who then polled about 300,000 votes, or slightly more than 3% of the total vote. As controversy over the coinage of silver (*see pp. 880–886*) began to supplant the paper-money issue, the Greenback Party declined in importance. Benjamin F. Butler (1818–1893) was the party's last Presidential candidate in 1884. He received nearly 134,000 votes, or 1.3% of the total vote. Most of the Greenbackers later joined the **People's Party** (*see*).

GUITEAU, Charles J. (1840?–1882). A religious fanatic and a disgruntled office seeker, Guiteau in 1881 shot and mortally wounded President **James A. Garfield** (*see*). Guiteau was raised in Freeport, Illinois, the son of a respectable Republican bank cashier. In 1860, he joined the Oneida Community, a collective farm in New York. Five years later, he went to New York City to draft plans for a chain of religious dailies, which never materialized. He eventually moved to Chicago, where he became a lawyer and worked as a debt collector, pocketing most of the money himself. During the 1880 Republican National Convention, Guiteau supported Ulysses S. Grant (1822–1885), the candidate of the antireform, or Stalwart, wing of the party. When Garfield was nominated, Guiteau sent Republican leaders a slightly altered version of a campaign speech he had written for Grant. The speech had never been used, but Guiteau believed that he deserved a political appointment for having written it. Shortly after Garfield's inauguration in March, 1881, Guiteau met with him at the White House and asked to be appointed the ambassador to France, or at least a consul in that nation. Garfield courteously refused the request. When Guiteau continued to pester the President, he was barred from the White House in May, 1881. Guiteau then wrote a threatening letter to Garfield and purchased a $15 bone-handled .44-caliber revolver, waiting for an opportunity to kill the President. At that time, there was no Secret Service to protect the President, only members of the Washington police force. Guiteau encountered Garfield on several occasions, but he apparently lost his nerve. However, on July 2, 1881, when Garfield arrived at the Baltimore and Potomac Railroad station in Washington, headed for Williams College in Massachusetts to make the commencement

address, Guiteau finally struck. He fired twice, crying, "I am a Stalwart and Arthur will be President!" Guiteau made no attempt to escape. On September 19, the President died from one of the wounds he had received, and **Chester A. Arthur** (*see*), the Vice-President, succeeded him. Guiteau's trial began on November 14 and lasted two and a half months. He remained convinced that his act had saved his party and his nation. Two men fired shots at Guiteau while he was in police custody—one was his prison guard, the other a man on horseback, who shot at Guiteau while he was being transported between the jail and the courtroom. The jury found Guiteau guilty, and he was hanged on June 30, 1881.

H

HARRIMAN, Edward Henry (1848–1909). One of America's greatest railroad executives, Harriman controlled a vast network of railroads, including the Union Pacific and Southern Pacific Railroads (*see pp. 872–873*). In 1901, in partnership with the banker Jacob Schiff (1847–1920) and backed by **John D. Rockefeller** (*see*), he was involved in the famous battle to gain control of the Northern Pacific Railroad from James J. Hill (1838–1916) and **J. P. Morgan** (*see*). Born in Long Island, Harriman, who began his career as a Wall Street stockbroker, became involved in his first important railroad venture in 1883 when he became a member of the directorate of the Illinois Central Railroad, whose finances he soon controlled. A director of the Union Pacific Railroad in 1897, Harriman became that line's executive-committee chairman the

following year. He expanded the Union Pacific, which, under his guidance, bought control of the Southern Pacific and Central Pacific Railroads in 1901. This gave Harriman an efficient West Coast rail system. His need for a line into Chicago at this time was the cause of his struggle with Hill and Morgan for the Northern Pacific. Neither side won, and a friendly settlement was reached in 1901 when the groups formed a holding company called the Northern Securities Company. Its control of the Great Northern, the Northern Pacific, and the Chicago, Burlington & Quincy—together with Harriman's control of the Union Pacific and Southern Pacific Railroads—gave it a virtual monopoly on the transportation facilities in the West. In 1904, in the first major test of the **Sherman Antitrust Act** (*see*) of 1890, the Supreme Court ordered the company dissolved. Harriman, however, subsequently increased his railroad holdings, and his policy of buying interests in numerous railroads led the Interstate Commerce Commission, which had been set up by the **Interstate Commerce Act** (*see*) of 1887, to investigate his railway operations in 1906–1907. The commission could not find a charge on which to prosecute Harriman, but it condemned his business practices. Harriman, whose other interests included the ownership of a steamship line to the Orient, was one of the founders of the Tompkins Square Boys' Club in New York in 1876, and he conducted a scientific expedition to Alaska in 1899. His son, William Averell Harriman (1891–1986) had a lengthy career in government service dating back to 1934. He was a governor of New York (1955–1958) and has served on the negotiating committee to end the war in Vietnam.

HARRISON, Benjamin (1833–1901). Harrison was elected the 23rd President of the United States in 1888, although he received nearly 100,000 popular votes fewer than his opponent, **Grover Cleveland** (*see*). His single term of office was marked by measures taken to try to protect

Benjamin Harrison

American trade and to improve Latin-American relations. Harrison, who was the grandson of the nation's ninth President, William Henry Harrison (1773–1841), was born in Ohio. He graduated from Miami University in Ohio in 1852. Two years later, he established a law practice in Indianapolis. The young, bearded lawyer soon became an active member of the Republican Party. In 1860, he was elected reporter for the Indiana supreme court. During the Civil War, Harrison helped to organize the 70th Indiana Volunteers. He rose from colonel of the regiment to brigadier general, but his reserved manner—he would later be referred to as a "human iceberg"

made him an unpopular commander. In 1876, Harrison was the unsuccessful candidate for governor of Indiana. Four years later, however, he was elected to the United States Senate. During his six years in the Senate (1881–1887), he aligned himself with the moderate element of his party but was conservative on economic matters. He supported a protective tariff, labor legislation, civil-service reform, and Civil War pensions. At the Republican National Convention in 1888, Harrison was nominated the party's Presidential candidate on the eighth ballot. In a notoriously corrupt campaign, Harrison's followers bought votes in Indiana and bribed members of New York's Tammany Hall to vote against their party's own candidate, Cleveland. Harrison defeated his Democratic opponent by getting 233 electoral votes to Cleveland's 168. Civil-service reform had been one of Harrison's campaign issues, but his Presidential efforts in that area were disappointing. In 1890, the **McKinley Tariff** (*see*) was enacted, which raised duties on imported manufactured goods to what was then the highest rate in the nation's history. That same year, Congress passed the **Sherman Silver Purchase Act** (*see*), which provided that the Treasury buy almost the entire output of the Western silver mines. The **Sherman Antitrust Act** (*see*) was also passed in 1890. In foreign affairs, Harrison encouraged the formation of the Pan-American Union, which held its first conference in Washington, D.C., in 1889. It was responsible for improved trade relations with Latin America. Running again against Cleveland in 1892, Harrison lost the support of many farmers in the Midwest because of his tariff policy. Most of them joined the newly formed **People's**

Party (*see*), which ran its own candidate, thus taking votes away from Harrison. He lost by 400,000 popular votes and received 145 electoral votes to Cleveland's 277. Harrison returned to his law practice in Indianapolis. He died on March 13, 1901.

HAYMARKET SQUARE RIOT.
A bitter dispute over the eight-hour working day between members of the **Knights of Labor** (*see*) and the McCormick Harvester Company preceded the riot in Chicago's Haymarket Square on May 4, 1886. On May 3, police summoned by the McCormick management had killed one man and injured several others during a fight between strikers and "scabs" (nonunion workers). A public meeting was called the following day at Haymarket Square to protest the incident. Ignoring the advice of the Chicago mayor, about 180 policemen tried to disperse the gathering of nearly 1,500 people. When a bomb, hurled into police ranks by an unidentified person, exploded, a riot broke out in which 11 persons, including seven policemen, were killed and more than 100 others injured. The press blamed "anarchists" for the violence. Of the 31 persons charged with being accessories to murder, eight were convicted. Four were hanged in 1887 and a fifth committed suicide in prison. The newly elected governor of Illinois, **John P. Altgeld** (*see*), who believed that their trial had been unfair, pardoned the remaining three prisoners in 1893. As a result of the riot, public sentiment turned against the Knights of Labor, seriously damaging the labor movement.

HENRY, Edward Lamson (1841–1919). Henry was an artist who chose for his subject matter American life and customs in the first half of the 19th century. Henry was educated in New York City, at the Pennsylvania Academy of Fine Arts, and in Paris. Working primarily in oils, Henry paid close attention to the details of everyday incidents and events (*see pp. 842–843*). His best-known works are "The Reception to Lafayette," "Off for the Races," and "Leaving at Early Morning in a Northeaster." He was elected to the National Academy of Design.

HOMESTEAD STRIKE. This bitter, four-month-long dispute between the workers and the management at the Homestead, Pennsylvania, plant of the Carnegie Steel Company began in violence in July, 1892. As a result of it, no steel union acquired substantial power in the industry for almost 40 years. The strike started when members of the Amalgamated Association of Iron and Steel Workers refused to accept a cut in wages that was intended to break the union. The company's general manager, **Henry Clay Frick** (*see*) —acting with the approval of its owner, Andrew Carnegie (1835–1919)—then locked out all union workers. He also hired 300 Pinkerton detectives to act as strikebreakers. On July 6, as two company barges guarded by Pinkerton men were being towed up the Monongahela River, enraged strikers started shooting at them. Thirteen men were killed in the battle that followed. Pennsylvania militiamen were called in on July 11 to aid the company. The strike was broken by November 21, but not before an anarchist, Alexander Berkman (1870–1936), had stabbed and shot Frick in an assassination attempt. The Amalgamated Association never regained power after the strike.

HOUSE OF MORGAN. *See* **Morgan, J. P.**

I

INTERSTATE COMMERCE ACT. The nation's first regulatory agency was set up in 1887 when Congress passed the Interstate Commerce Act to regulate commerce between the states. The act required railroads engaged in interstate business to charge "reasonable and just" rates. It specifically prohibited discriminatory rates, rebates, and pooling operations. Charging more for a short haul than for a long one on the same road was also made illegal. The act established the five-member Interstate Commerce Commission to investigate the management of railroads, review company papers and books, and call witnesses. However, the commission was not authorized to fix rates, and its rulings were not binding. It therefore was obliged to depend on the courts for enforcement of its orders. Because most courts were partial to big business during the 1890s, the commission failed to provide effective railroad regulation. By 1898, it did little more than collect and publish railway statistics. Later, the Elkins Act (1903), the Hepburn Act (1906), the Mann-Elkins Act (1910), and other legislation increased the commission's power and widened its jurisdiction to include other carriers of interstate commerce.

J

JAMES, Jesse Woodson (1847–1882). This notorious gunman was the leader of a gang of bandits who committed spectacular bank and train robberies in the Midwest for more than 15 years. James was raised on a Missouri farm. He was 14 years old when, at the outbreak of the Civil War, he and his

older brother, Alexander Franklin ("Frank") James (1843–1915), joined the guerrilla troops of the Confederate raider William Quantrill(1837–1865). They fought with him until the close of the war in 1865. The following year, Jesse organized an outlaw band with **Coleman Younger** (*see*) and his brothers. During the next 15

Jesse James

years, the gang was credited with holding up three stagecoaches, seven trains, and 11 banks. At least 16 men were killed during their robberies. In 1876, the gang attempted to hold up a bank at Northfield, Minnesota. The robbery turned into a shooting spree, during which three of the outlaws were killed and the three Younger brothers were wounded and captured. Jesse and Frank went into hiding for the next three years. Then the James brothers struck again—three more trains were robbed between 1879 and 1881. The governor of Missouri, Thomas Crittenden (1832–1909), offered a $10,000 reward for Jesse, dead or alive. Lured by the offer, two members of his gang—Robert Ford and his brother Charles— turned traitor. Robert shot Jesse in the back of the head on April 3, 1882, in St. Joseph, Missouri.

Both Fords later pleaded guilty to charges of murder and were sentenced to hang. However, the governor unconditionally pardoned both men, and they finally received $500 in reward money. Although he had been a cold-blooded killer, after his death the legend grew that Jesse had been a hero who, like Robin Hood, stole from the rich and gave to the poor. There is no evidence to support this legend.

K

KANE, John (1860–1934). Kane was a Pennsylvania artist known for his primitive style of painting. Born in Scotland, he immigrated to America in 1879. He settled in the Pittsburgh area, where he found work as a street paver, house painter, and mill hand. Painting in his spare time, Kane developed a style characterized by simple patterns, bright colors, and careful detail. Among the subjects Kane painted were the steel mills on the banks of the Monongahela River (*see p. 820*).

KELLEY, Oliver Hudson (1826–1913). Kelley was the principal founder of the **Granges** (*see*), a national organization of farmers that developed in the 1870s. Kelley moved to the Midwest from his native Massachusetts and began farming in Minnesota in 1849. Fifteen years later, he returned east, taking a position as a clerk in the Bureau of Agriculture in Washington. In 1865, he toured Minnesota on an agricultural survey for the bureau. While on a similar tour of the South the following year, he conceived the idea of organizing farmers into a fraternal and social association. With six others, Kelley founded the National Grange of the Patrons of Husbandry in 1867. As originally conceived, the association was nonpolitical. Its goal was to be the expansion of farmers' social and educational opportunities. Like "an engine with too much steam on all the time," Kelley set out to establish Granges across America. Because the movement was slow in growing, Kelley redefined its objectives. The establishment of cooperatives and the breakup of railroad monopolies were then stressed as its primary concerns. Farmers at that time believed they were being victimized by high interest rates and unfair railroad freight costs. So many joined the movement that by 1874 more than 20,000 Granges had been established, the majority of them in the South and the Midwest. However, membership fell off sharply as several new political organizations, such as the **Greenback Party** and the **People's Party** (*see both*), attracted increasing numbers of farmers. Kelley, who had moved to Florida in 1875, resigned as secretary of the Grange three years later. He dealt in land speculation before returning to Washington. His only book, *Origin and Progress of the Order of the Patrons of Husbandry,* was published in 1875.

KNIGHTS OF LABOR. Founded in 1869 by **Uriah S. Stephens** (*see*), the Knights of Labor claimed nearly 700,000 men and women members when it was the dominant labor organization in America in the late 1880s. First called the Noble and Holy Order of the Knights of Labor, the order had many secret rituals with religious overtones and was primarily made up of skilled workers in a variety of crafts. However, after 1878, when Stephens was replaced by Terence V. Powderly (1849–1924) as the Grand Master Workman, the union became national in scope and accepted as members unskilled workers and even employers. Only bankers, lawyers, gamblers, stockbrokers, and saloon keepers were excluded. Physicians were allowed to join in 1881 and black workers two years later. The union's motto was, "An injury to one is the concern of all." In 1881, over Stephens' objections, the secrecy was abandoned, and the union grew rapidly. The aims of the union included an eight-hour working day, the abolition of child labor, and industrial safety measures. Although the union did sponsor strikes, boycotts were preferred as an economic weapon. After the membership rolls reached their peak in 1886, the Knights began to lose strength, chiefly because of several strikes that year and the fact that newspapers unjustly blamed the Knights for causing the **Haymarket Square riot** (*see*). In addition, the **American Federation of Labor** (*see*), a union organized on a craft basis, was attracting craftsmen away from the Knights. The economic depression following the **Panic of 1893** (*see*) ended the union's importance. The organization was formally terminated in 1917.

L

LAZARUS, Emma (1849–1887). This poet expressed her faith in America as a home for the oppressed by writing the inspiring words inscribed on the pedestal of the **Statue of Liberty** (*see*). Miss Lazarus was born in New York City to a wealthy Jewish family and educated by private tutors. She published her first volume of verses at the age of 17 and immediately won the esteem and friendship of Ralph Waldo Emerson (1803–1882). Although she was not religious, the persecution of Jews in Russia in the early

1880s transformed her from a lady of letters into a dedicated champion of her people. When in 1881 Russian refugees began arriving in droves at Ward's Island in New York, then a United States port of entry for immigrants, Emma worked to aid them. She commemorated the plight of the Russian Jew in an impassioned volume of poetry entitled *Songs of a Semite,* published in 1882. Her sonnet, "The New Colossus," part of which appears on the Statue of Liberty's pedestal, was written in 1883. The words were engraved there in 1886, only a year before Miss Lazarus died at the age of 38:

> *. . . Give me your tired, your poor,*
> *Your huddled masses yearning to breathe free,*
> *The wretched refuse of your teeming shore,*
> *Send these, the homeless, tempest-tossed, to me:*
> *I lift my lamp beside the golden door.*

LEASE, Mary Elizabeth (1853–1933). Known as the Kansas Pythoness, this fiery agrarian reformer of the late 19th century is best remembered for her exhortation to farmers to "raise less corn and more Hell." Mary was born in Ridgway, Pennsylvania, and moved to Kansas in 1860. She married Charles L. Lease in 1873 and was admitted to the Kansas bar about 12 years later. Because her father had been a political exile from Ireland, she made speeches for the cause of Irish independence in the mid-1880s and became a local celebrity. People called her Mary Ellen or Mary Yellin. Mrs. Lease entered politics in 1888 by running for a county post on the Union Labor Party ticket. However, she lost the contest. During the national elections of 1890, she became a leader in the **People's Party** (*see*) and made 160 speeches in the campaign. When the Populists came to power in Kansas in 1893, she served as president of the State Board of Charities and representative to the World's Columbian Exposition at Chicago. Her aspirations to become the governor, a Senator, and then the President were thwarted by the decline of the Populists in Kansas, and in 1896 she moved to New York. There she wrote for the *World,* owned by **Joseph Pulitzer** (*see*). Mrs. Lease crusaded for women's suffrage, prohibition, the popular election of Senators, "free silver," and birth control until she retired in 1918.

LIBERAL REPUBLICAN PARTY. Dissatisfied with the policies of President Ulysses S. Grant (1822–1885) and angered by the rampant corruption of Grant's first administration, a small body of influential men broke with the main Republican organization and founded the Liberal Republican Party in 1872. Among the leaders of the new party were Horace Greeley (1811–1872), the editor of the New York *Tribune;* Charles Francis Adams (1807–1886), a former minister to Britain; Senator Charles Sumner (1811–1874) of Massachusetts; and two Missouri liberals who had defeated regular Republicans in the election of 1870—Senator **Carl Schurz** (*see*) and Benjamin Gratz Brown (1826–1885). Meeting at Cincinnati in May, 1872, the party nominated Greeley for President and Brown for Vice-President. It adopted a platform calling for a merit-based civil-service system and an end to exploitation of the South under Reconstruction. The diverse membership of the new party forced it to adopt a neutral position on tariffs. The Democratic Party, convening at Baltimore in July, found itself without a candidate strong enough to challenge Grant and thus endorsed the Liberal Republican ticket. Despite this dual support, Greeley was soundly beaten in the November election by Grant, whose plurality was almost 800,000 votes. After this defeat, the Liberal Republican Party—never more than a loose coalition—rapidly disbanded. Nevertheless, it had proved an important influence in creating pressure for civil-service reform (*see* **Pendleton Act**) and a more lenient policy toward the former Confederate States.

LLOYD, Henry D. (1847–1903). A social reformer and union organizer, Lloyd wrote several books condemning business trusts and demanding justice for the workingman. Lloyd, who had graduated from Columbia College in 1869, joined the Chicago *Tribune* three years later as the financial editor and an editorial writer. His first exposé—focused on the methods of the vast Standard Oil Company of **John D. Rockefeller** (*see*)—was published in 1881 in the *Atlantic Monthly.* Four years later, Lloyd resigned from the newspaper to devote all his time to publicizing the social problems caused by similar trusts. He called his first book, about a strike by coal miners, *A Strike of Millionaires against Miners* (1890). His most important book was *Wealth Against Commonwealth* (1894). This book, which was compiled from court records and legislative inquiries, was a devastating account of the history and growth of trusts, with particular emphasis on the Standard Oil Company. Throughout his career, Lloyd not only wrote but also became directly involved in industrial conflicts. He helped to organize Milwaukee streetcar workers, worked to secure commuted sentences for two men involved in the **Hay-**

market Square riot (*see*), and supported the conduct of **Eugene V. Debs** in the **Pullman strike** (*see both*). Lloyd waited until 1903 to join the Socialist Party, although he had earlier supported its programs to abolish trusts and emancipate the workingman. At the time of his death, he was campaigning for the municipal ownership of streetcars in Chicago.

M

McKINLEY TARIFF. The McKinley Tariff of 1890 was the highest protective tariff enacted in American history up to that time. It was named after Representative William McKinley (1843–1901) of Ohio, the chairman of the House Ways and Means Committee. Passed in October, 1890, the tariff raised duties on imports to an average of 48.4%. In order to gain the votes of Western Congressmen for the passage of the McKinley Tariff, Eastern interests supported the **Sherman Silver Purchase Act** (*see*). Among the goods affected by the tariff were woolens, wool, and barley. The act also increased the number of duty-free imports. Included on the free list were sugar, molasses, coffee, and hides. Under the act, however, the federal government paid American sugar growers a bounty of 2¢ a pound for all home-grown sugar. This allowed them to undersell Hawaiian growers and caused an economic depression in the islands. The tariff sought not only to protect already established industries but also to nourish "infant" industries and to create new ones. Accordingly, a duty was put on tin plate—to be removed within six years if the industry failed to develop. Another feature of the act was a reciprocity clause. It authorized the President to ter-

minate the free importation of certain goods from other nations if duties imposed by those nations on American-manufactured exports were considered unjust. The effect of the McKinley Tariff was to increase consumer prices and decrease federal revenues. The unpopular act was instrumental in causing the Republican defeat in the elections of 1892. During the **Panic of 1893** (*see*), the act was criticized for discouraging trade and fostering unemployment. It was superseded in 1894 by the **Wilson-Gorman Tariff** (*see*), which was intended to lower tariff rates.

MERGENTHALER, Ottmar (1854–1899). Mergenthaler's invention of the Linotype in 1884 mechanized the setting of printing type and revolutionized the publishing industry. Born in Germany, Mergenthaler was apprenticed to a watchmaker at the age of 14 and immigrated to the United States in 1872 to avoid being drafted into the German army. After four years in Washington, D.C., he moved to Baltimore and worked in a scientific-instrument shop. In connection with his work, Mergenthaler was asked to correct the defects in a machine that was intended to eliminate the setting of type by hand. When he was unable to do so, he began experimenting with designs for his own machine. The Linotype, which casts metal lines of type, was first used on July 3, 1886, in the composing room of the New York *Tribune*. The invention made feasible a vast expansion in the publishing industry. By 1895, more than 3,100 Linotype machines were in use in the United States. Mergenthaler continued to work on his machine, devising more than 50 patented improvements before his death.

MORGAN, John Pierpont (1837–1913). By reorganizing and consolidating American railroads and industry during the late 1800s, Morgan became the foremost financial power of his day (*see pp. 868–869*). A native of Hartford, Connecticut, "J. P." was educated abroad and in 1856 was apprenticed to the London branch of his father's investment-banking firm. He later managed the company's New York operations. Morgan's

BROWN BROTHERS

J. P. Morgan

rise to prominence began in 1869 when he seized control of the Albany & Susquehanna Railroad from **Jay Gould** and **James Fisk** (*see both*). At the time of the **Panic of 1873** (*see*), Morgan began lending money to the government. Following the **Panic of 1893** (*see*), Morgan gained control of the largest single group of railroads in America. As he did with his other business enterprises, he exercised his control by personally appointing the trustees who managed the voting stock. He founded J. P. Morgan & Company, which was popularly known as the House of Morgan, in 1895. This banking firm obtained European capital for American industry and financed enterprises ranging from mining and manufacturing to shipping lines and insurance companies. In 1901, Morgan bought out Andrew Carnegie (1835–1919) for $492,000,000 and established what was then the largest corporation in the world, United States Steel. During the Panic of 1907, both the government and business turned to him to stabilize the financial situation. He organized loans for banks and the federal government and decided what banks should close because they were insolvent. Morgan's dominance of 47 corporations and 72 directorates led in 1912 to a Congressional investigation. He defended himself in public, but he refused to disclose the resources of J. P. Morgan & Company. After his death in Rome on March 31, 1913, his estate was estimated to be worth more than $68,000,000, and his art treasures were valued at $50,000,000 more. Morgan's renowned collection of paintings is now in New York City's Metropolitan Museum of Art. The rare books he collected are on view in a library next to his former mansion in the same city.

MORRILL TARIFF. The Morrill Tariff inaugurated a 70-year period of high protective import duties. The tariff, passed by the Republican-controlled House in May, 1860, was enacted in March, 1861, after the secession of seven Southern states. It was named for Representative Justin S. Morrill (1810–1898) of Vermont, the chairman of the House Ways and Means Committee. The act increased rates from 5% to 10%. Materials covered included iron and wool. Subsequent revisions of the Morrill Tariff raised duties from an average rate of 18.8% in 1861 to an average of 47% in 1869. The purpose of the tariff was to protect the nation's new industries from lower-priced foreign products and to induce Pennsylvania and other industrial states to support Abraham Lincoln (1809–1865) and the Republican Party in the 1860 election. The rates were later raised to compensate manufacturers for the high taxes needed to pay the costs of the Civil War. The Morrill Tariff was superseded by the tariffs of 1870, 1872, and 1883, all of which slightly reduced rates.

MUGWUMPS. When the Republican National Convention nominated **James G. Blaine** (*see*) for President in 1884, many reformers, who regarded Blaine as a corrupt politician, bolted the party to back the Democratic nominee, **Grover Cleveland** (*see*). These defectors were derisively branded "Mugwumps," an Indian term derived from the Algonquian word *mugwomp,* meaning "captain" or "chief." They played an influential part in Blaine's defeat. Among the best known of the Mugwumps were cartoonist Thomas Nast (1840–1902), the Reverend Henry Ward Beecher (1813–1887), and **Carl Schurz** (*see*). The term "Mugwump" has been revived from time to time to apply to political mavericks such as Theodore Roosevelt (1858–1919), who left the Republican ranks in 1912 to form the Progressive Party.

N

NATIONAL FARMERS' ALLIANCE. This powerful organization, also known as the Northern or Northwestern Alliance, waged campaigns for agrarian reforms after the decline of the **Granges** and the **Greenback Party** (*see both*) in the late 19th century. Formed in 1880 by Milton George, the editor of a Chicago journal entitled *The Western Rural,* the National Farmers' Alliance was created to improve the lot of the many farmers who were then faced with declining prices for their produce, high interest and mortgage rates, and excessive freight charges by railroads. Within a year, the organization had 1,000 members, and it soon became a loose federation of state and local chapters throughout the Midwest. By the late 1880s, hundreds of thousands had joined the alliance. Although it sponsored business, cultural, and social programs, the organization gained national attention when it ran reform candidates for state and local offices. During its 1889 convention in St. Louis—at which the keynote speaker was the agrarian reformer **Mary Elizabeth Lease** (*see*)—the nation's major labor unions announced their support of the federation. The following year, the alliance ran third-party tickets in state and local elections and succeeded in winning many races. In the local elections of 1892, the political functions of the National Farmers' Alliance were largely taken over by the **People's Party** (*see*), with which it became identified. A similar organization, the National Farmers' Alliance and Industrial Union, was founded in Texas in 1874 and gained strength after 1886. It was based in the South and had a strong centralized organization. It and its Northern counterpart, however, were never able to agree to a merger. Both organizations declined after the defeat of **William Jennings Bryan** (*see*), the Democratic-Populist candidate for President in 1896.

NEW IMMIGRATION. Many emigrants from eastern and southern Europe began to arrive in America in the 1880s. By the time this new wave of settlers—or New Immigration, as it was called— was over in the 1920s, more than 20,000,000 had reached the nation's shores. During the so-called Old Immigration of 1820–1880, the majority of settlers had come from the nations of western and northern Europe—Britain, Ireland, Germany, and Scandinavia. In the 1880s, however, large numbers of emigrants began to arrive from Russia, Italy, Poland, Austria-Hungary, and the Balkans. The majority concentrated in the large industrial cities, where fac- tory jobs were available. The Russians and Italians settled princi- pally in New York City. The Poles, Hungarians, and Czechs formed ethnic blocs in the industrial Mid- west, especially Chicago. Many Chinese also arrived, chiefly to work in building railroads, until the **Chinese Exclusion Act** (*see*) of 1882 prohibited their entry. Most of the newcomers were attracted by the opportunity to make a bet- ter life in the United States. In- dustrial expansion and the open- ing of new territories in America offered hope of a higher standard of living than that prevailing in Europe. Others, like the Russian Jews, were fleeing religious per- secution. Many of the immigrants were persuaded to come by agents of railroad and steamship com- panies who recruited settlers in Europe. Rate wars between the various transportation companies made the trip relatively inexpen- sive. At the turn of the century, the fare for the Atlantic crossing —in steerage—was only $30. The peak immigration year was 1907, during which 1,285,349 newcom- ers arrived. After 1892, most of the immigrants passed through **Ellis Island** (*see*), the principal United States receiving station. The flow of immigrants to Amer- ica was drastically reduced after 1924 with the passage of the re- strictive Johnson-Reed Act.

P

PACIFIC RAILWAY ACTS. The Pacific Railway Acts were two laws passed by Congress—the first in 1862 and the second in 1864—to encourage the construc- tion of railroads in the West, in particular the first transcontinen- tal railroad, which was built jointly by the Union Pacific and Central Pacific Railroads (*see p. 821*). The first act authorized the Central

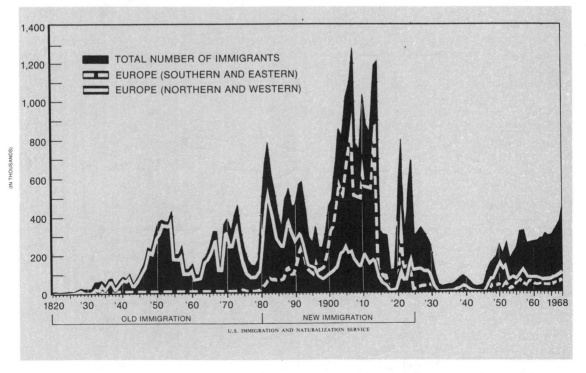

During the New Immigration, 20,000,000 settlers came to America, the largest influx of foreigners in the nation's history.

Pacific to lay tracks eastward from Sacramento, California, while the Union Pacific was to build westward from Omaha, Nebraska. The two lines were finally linked on May 10, 1869, at Promontory, Utah (*see pp. 834–835*). The act of 1862 also made generous land grants and loans to the construction companies involved. The second act doubled these grants to offer the building corporations further incentive. The speculation stimulated by these acts caused several scandals, the most notorious of which was the **Credit Mobilier Scandal** (*see*).

PANIC OF 1873. One of America's most serious financial disasters, the Panic of 1873 caused a major economic depression that was accompanied by widespread strikes, notably against the nation's railroads (*see pp. 828–829*). Following the Civil War, American finances had been shaken by unrestrained railroad speculation —such as the **Credit Mobilier scandal** (*see*). In addition, there had been unsound investment schemes in many fields and inflation, and the nation's imports were exceeding its exports. The panic was precipitated by the failure, on September 18, 1873, of the Philadelphia banking house of Jay Cooke and Company. Jay Cooke (1821–1905), at that time America's most famous financier, was forced into bankruptcy when he failed to raise $100,000,000 to finance the second transcontinental railroad, the Northern Pacific. After his firm closed its doors, 37 New York banks and brokerage houses followed suit, and the New York Stock Exchange closed for the next 10 days. By the end of the year, more than 5,000 businesses had also failed. In the wake of the disaster, more than 18,000 commercial enterprises went bankrupt between 1876 and 1877. Most

railroads also went bankrupt, industries—including two-thirds of the nation's iron mills and furnaces—shut down, unemployment was high, and a widespread reduction in wages caused strikes and violence. The lack of organized public relief for the poor and the federal government's use of force to put down strikes created distrust between labor and the government that lasted for many years. The depression began to subside in 1878, and the economy began to improve until the **Panic of 1883** (*see*).

PANIC OF 1883. The Panic of 1883, a financial depression that lasted for two years, was mild in comparison to the **Panic of 1873** and the **Panic of 1893** (*see both*). Beginning as a minor recession, the Panic of 1883 was prolonged because of an economic crisis stemming from the overexpansion of railroad building in the early 1880s. These years were also marked by widespread agitation for an eight-hour working day, which led to the **Haymarket Square riot** (*see*) of 1886. The Panic of 1883 was followed by a period of quick recovery (1885–1890), a

brief recession (1890–1891), and another recovery (1892) before the nation was hit by the devastating Panic of 1893.

PANIC OF 1893. One of the worst financial disasters of the 19th century, the Panic of 1893 was followed by a depression that lasted for four years. The overexpansion in railroad building and industrial development during the 1880s and early 1890s, as well as an agricultural depression beginning in 1887, were the general causes of the panic. Its specific causes included the failure in November, 1890, of the British banking house of Baring Brothers. This led foreign investors to sell their American securities and caused a serious drain of gold from the United States. In addition, the **McKinley Tariff** (*see*) of 1890 resulted in a reduction of the annual revenue received from tariff duties, and the **Sherman Silver Purchase Act** (*see*) of 1890 contributed to the drain of gold from the United States Treasury. By the winter of 1892–1893, these factors created a widespread fear that the United States would be forced off the gold standard. Peo-

Harrison bids adieu to Cleveland, leaving behind a depleted Treasury—and a panic.

ple began to hoard gold, and European investors again began to sell their American securities and to demand payments in gold. A hint of the impending disaster came in February, 1893, with the failure of the Philadelphia & Reading Railroad. The following April, the American gold reserve fell below the $100,000,000 mark, which was considered the minimum amount of gold necessary to support the paper money in circulation. By the end of 1893, more than 600 banks, nearly 15,000 businesses, and many railroads had failed, and the gold reserve had fallen to $80,000,000. The repeal of the Sherman Act in November, 1893, helped to check the stock-market panic, but the Treasury's gold reserve continued to shrink and the depression became worse. Unemployment rose, and in the spring of 1894 a group of jobless men led by **Jacob Coxey** (*see*) staged a march on Washington, D.C., to demand relief. The depression finally subsided in 1897 when crops in Europe were so poor that America was able to export large quantities of its agricultural produce, for which it was paid in badly needed gold. Prices then began to rise, and financial conditions improved.

PATRONS OF HUSBANDRY.
See **Granges.**

PENDLETON, George Hunt (1825–1889). As chairman of the Senate committee on civil service, Pendleton sponsored the nation's first significant civil-service reform act, the **Pendleton Act** (*see*) of 1883. Known as Gentleman George because of his dignified manner, Pendleton was born in Cincinnati and became a lawyer in 1847. After a term (1854–1856) in the Ohio senate, he was elected to the House of Representatives (1857–1865). During the Civil

George H. Pendleton

War, Pendleton was a prominent Peace Democrat. In 1864, he was the Vice-Presidential candidate on the Democratic ticket headed by George B. McClellan (1826–1885). Pendleton favored the payment of government bonds in greenbacks rather than specie (gold or silver). This view cost him the support of the Eastern wing of the Democratic Party and probably, as a result, the Presidential nomination in 1868. The next year, he ran for governor of Ohio but lost to Rutherford B. Hayes (1822–1893). Pendleton retired from politics for the next 10 years, serving instead as president of the Kentucky Central Railroad. In 1878, the Ohio legislature elected him to the Senate (1879–1885). The act that bears his name was drafted by Dorman Eaton (1823–1899), who headed the National Civil Service Commission. It was designed to protect federal officeholders from losing their jobs because of party politics. Pendleton's support of the bill irritated those in his party who still favored the spoils system, and Pendleton was defeated for reelection in 1884. President **Grover Cleveland** (*see*) appointed him minister to Germany in 1885, and he served in that capacity until his death.

PENDLETON ACT. Signed by President **Chester A. Arthur** (*see*) in 1883, the Pendleton Act set up a merit system to protect federal officeholders from losing their jobs because of partisan politics. Prior to the act's passage, politicians had used the spoils system to maintain party strength. Election winners removed as many officeholders as possible, replacing them with loyal party supporters. In 1871, Senator **Carl Schurz** (*see*) of Missouri sponsored a law establishing a Civil Service Commission. The commission was headed at the beginning by reformer George W. Curtis (1824–1892), but it lasted only a few years because politicians opposed its attempts to correct the abuses. However, the assassination of President **James A. Garfield** (*see*) in 1881 by a disappointed office seeker resulted in demands by the public for reform. A bill written by Dorman Eaton (1823–1899), who had also headed the defunct commission, and sponsored by Senator **George H. Pendleton** (*see*) of Ohio passed the House and Senate by wide margins. It established a new Civil Service Commission, with three commissioners appointed by the President. Only two commissioners could be from the same political party. They were given the authority to draw up competitive examinations to determine the fitness of job applicants. The practice of assessing federal office-holders for campaign contributions, formerly a common practice, was prohibited. The act also stated that no federal employee could be fired for purely political reasons. Only 12% of all federal employees were placed under the jurisdiction of the commission, but the President was given powers to extend the coverage. Currently, more than 90% of all federal employees are protected by civil service.

PEOPLE'S PARTY. Discontent among poor farmers in the West and the South led to the organization of the People's Party of America (known in some states as the Populist Party) in the early 1890s, shortly after the breakup of the **Greenback Party** (*see*). The first national convention of the People's Party—held in July, 1892, at Omaha, Nebraska—nominated former Greenbacker **James B. Weaver** (*see*) to run for President. The Populist platform called for increasing the amount of money in circulation by the unlimited coinage of silver, government ownership of railroads and telegraph and telephone systems, a graduated income tax, the direct election of United States Senators, and the exclusion of foreigners from owning land in America. In addition, in an effort to secure the backing of city workers, the Populists committed themselves to the support of an eight-hour working day and of restrictions on immigration. Weaver received more than 1,000,000 votes in the 1892 election, and the Populists hoped for victory four years later. However, when the Democrats nominated a "free-silver" advocate, **William Jennings Bryan** (*see*), in 1896, the People's Party decided to endorse his candidacy (although it put forward its own Vice-Presidential contender). The gradual return of prosperity following the **Panic of 1893** (*see*) and the fact that many of its programs were adopted by the Democratic and Republican Parties caused the People's Party to diminish in strength after 1896. By 1904, it was only a token organization.

PLESSY VS. FERGUSON. This

Supreme Court case constitutionally established the "separate but equal" doctrine of segregation of blacks and whites. The case was the result of a Louisiana law of 1890 requiring railroads to provide "equal but separate accommodations for the white and colored races." Following the Civil War, Southern states had tried to limit the legal and social rights of blacks by means of Black Codes. This effort was only temporarily checked by the passage of the Fourteenth and Fifteenth Amendments during the Reconstruction Era. In June, 1892, a young mulatto named Homer Adolph Plessy decided to test the Louisiana statute. He boarded a train and took a seat in the white car. When the conductor asked him to move to the black coach, he refused and was arrested. Later, Judge John H. Ferguson of New Orleans overruled Plessy's plea that the Louisiana law was null and void because it was unconstitutional. Plessy subsequently appealed to the United States Supreme Court, which handed down its opinion on May 18, 1896. The decision, which was delivered by Justice Henry Brown (1836–1913), upheld the constitutionality of the "separate but equal" doctrine. The Court majority said that accommodations could be equal without being identical. Justice John M. Harlan (1833–1911), in a famous dissenting opinion, declared that the "separate but equal" law violated both the Thirteenth Amendment, which outlaws slavery, as well as the Fourteenth, which guarantees equal protection under the law. For more than 50 years afterward, federal and state courts cited *Plessy vs. Ferguson* when they ruled on Jim Crow legislation. The doctrine was not reversed until May 17, 1954, when the Supreme Court, in *Brown et al. vs. Board of Education of Topeka et al.,* declared that all segregation in public schools was "inherently unequal," and that legislation barring blacks from attending school with whites violated the Fourteenth Amendment.

POPULISTS. *See* **People's Party.**

PULLMAN, George Mortimer (1831–1897). A cabinetmaker and contractor born in upstate New York, Pullman designed the railway sleeping car that bears his name and that is now used all over the world. Pullman moved to Chicago in 1855 and three years later remodeled into sleeping cars two day coaches owned by the Chicago & Alton Railroad. These cars were put into service immediately, but other railroads were reluctant to adopt them. Despite his initial failure, Pullman improved the design of his original sleeping cars and in 1864, together with a friend, Ben Field, began to build the "Pioneer," his first railroad car specifically designed as a sleeper. The car, which was completed the following year, included an upper berth that folded up during the day and a lower berth that converted into a standard coach seat. It also had an attractive interior decor, as well as improved lighting, ventilating, and heating facilities. The "Pioneer," whose berth arrangements are very similar to those found in modern Pullman cars, was an enormous success. In 1867, Pullman and Field merged with the company founded by their competitor, **T. T. Woodruff** (*see*), to form the Pullman Palace Car Company. The company's cars were purchased by most of America's major railroads and revolutionized railway travel throughout the world. Pullman and his friend Field designed a dining car in 1868, a chair car (*see p. 841*) in 1875, and a vestibule car in 1887 and also built many private railway cars for rich people. Their company soon became the largest of its type in the world, with plants all over America. In 1880–1881, Pullman founded the town of Pullman, Illinois, which was incorporated

George M. Pullman

with Chicago in 1889. A planned community, it contained a car-manufacturing plant and housing for the company's employees and was considered America's healthiest industrial town. The community was the scene of the famous **Pullman strike** (*see*) in May, 1894. George Pullman was also the president of an elevated passenger railway in New York City.

PULLMAN STRIKE. One of the most serious labor disputes of the late 19th century, the Pullman strike began as a walkout staged by the employees of the Pullman Palace Car Company in May, 1894. It soon developed into a nationwide railway strike marked by mob violence. In the wake of a serious depression following the **Panic of 1893** (*see*), the Pullman company had cut the wages of its workers by about 25%. However, it had not reduced the rent or the prices it charged its workers in company-run stores in the town of

Pullman. This community which had recently become part of Chicago was founded by **George Pullman** (*see*) for the employees of the company's chief manufacturing plant, who lived and worked there. After protesting without success, many of them joined the American Railway Union under the leadership of **Eugene V. Debs** (*see*) in the spring of 1894. On May 11, about 2,500 employees in the Pullman plant stopped working, forcing it to shut down. When mediation efforts to settle the strike failed, the union staged a nationwide boycott of Pullman cars. Because these cars were used by most major railroads, the boycott resulted in a virtual shutdown of the nation's railways by June 30. The strikers ignored a federal injunction on July 2 forbidding them to interfere with the trains, and two days later President **Grover Cleveland** (*see*) ordered federal troops to Chicago to enforce the injunction (*see pp. 828–830*). The arrival of mounted forces touched off mob violence and the destruction of railway property in Chicago and other cities throughout the nation. Within several days, Debs was arrested for violating the injunction, and soon some trains began running under military protection. On July 20, the troops left Chicago, and the strike ended. The Pullman strike led to a campaign to curb the government's increasing use of labor injunctions. In 1898, Congress passed the Erdman Act, the first of a long series of laws that provided for the settlement of labor disputes through arbitration.

R

RAUSCHENBUSCH, Walter (1861–1918). This influential Baptist minister devised and preached a "social gospel" to make the

teachings of Jesus relevant to the social problems existing in America during the late 1800s. The son of German immigrant parents, Rauschenbusch was born in Rochester, New York, and educated in both the United States and Germany. After graduating from Rochester Theological Seminary in 1886, he accepted a pastorate with the Second German Baptist Church in New York City and remained there 11 years. While serving in this parish, he learned about the condition of the working classes and showed an interest in socialism. It was during the depression following the **Panic of 1893** (*see*) that Rauschenbusch came to believe that traditional religious teachings "didn't fit" with the realities of contemporary life. He preached that social consciousness should be an important concern of Christians and that they should strive to alleviate the conditions that create city slums and cause enmity between workers and employers. He attacked child labor, bad working conditions, and inadequate wages. In 1897, Rauschenbusch began teaching New Testament interpretation in the German department of Rochester Theological Seminary, and from 1902 until his death he was professor of church history there. As one of the nation's leading proponents of Christian socialism, Rauschenbusch explained his views in lectures, articles, and such books as *Christianity and the Social Crisis* (1907).

REVELS, Hiram Rhoades (1822–1901). This black clergyman and educator filled out the unexpired Senate term of Confederate President Jefferson Davis (1808–1889) and later worked to rid Mississippi of carpetbaggers. Revels was born to free parents in Fayetteville, North Carolina. After working as a barber in his home state, Revels attended schools in Indiana and Ohio in 1844. The following year, he became a minister of the African Methodist Episcopal Church. He did missionary work among blacks in the Midwest and then accepted a church post in Baltimore. Later, he became principal of a school there for blacks. During the Civil War, Revels helped recruit black regiments in Maryland and Missouri and served as chaplain in one made up of freed slaves from Mississippi. After the war, he settled in Natchez, where he continued his religious activities. Although Revels sought to avoid racial tension with the white people of the state, he was finally persuaded to enter local politics. In 1870, Revels went to Washington to fill the Senate seat to which the unreconstructed Mississippi legislature had elected Davis in 1865. Nominally a Republican, Revels won a reputation for his conservative views and opposed the Radical Republicans then in Congress. After his term expired in 1871, Revels returned to Mississippi and became president of Alcorn University, a recently opened institution for freedmen. In 1875, he helped the Mississippi Democrats rid the state of carpetbaggers. In explaining his actions in a letter to President Ulysses S. Grant (1822–1885), Revels said that all good Mississippians had joined in the cause. The following year, Revels became editor of the *Southwestern Christian Advocate*.

ROCKEFELLER, John Davison (1839–1937). Rockefeller was a New York-born industrialist and philanthropist who founded an oil empire and made his name synonymous with great wealth (*see pp. 870–871*). After moving to Ohio in 1853, Rockefeller worked hard and lived frugally, and in 1863 he established an oil refinery in Cleveland. In 1870, this company became the Standard Oil Company of Ohio, and within a decade it dominated American and foreign oil markets. In 1882, the company's holdings were organized into the Standard Oil Trust, which was dissolved 10 years later by a court order because of its monopoly over the oil industry. Its successor was Standard Oil of New Jersey, a holding company organized in 1899. It was ordered dissolved by the Supreme Court two years later in a famous antitrust case. The company was subsequently reorganized and still retains control over vast oil interests. Rockefeller, who retired from business in 1911, was also involved in the banking, railroad, and insurance fields and was a director of the United States Steel Corporation after its formation in 1901. With a personal fortune amounting to more than $1,000,000,000, Rockefeller liked to give away dimes to hard-working people he encountered while walking on the street. During the 1890s, he became involved in numerous philanthropic activities, including the founding of the University of Chicago (1892), the Rockefeller Institute for Medical Research (1901), and the Rockefeller Foundation (1913). In all, he gave more than $550,000,000 to establishing these institutions. Rockefeller's descendants continued the tradition of combining business and public service. His grandsons have included two who were elected governors of their states—Nelson A. Rockefeller (1908–1979) of New York and Winthrop Rockefeller (1912–1973) of Arkansas, both Republicans. Nelson Rockefeller also served as Vice-President in the administration of President Gerald R. Ford. A third grandson, Laurence S. Rockefeller (born 1910), became noted as a conservationist.

S

SCHURZ, Carl (1829–1906). Throughout his career in public life, Schurz was respected as a man of conscience who remained true to his principles in spite of the political consequences. Born in Germany, he was a student leader in the revolutionary uprisings of 1848–1849 and was forced to leave the country. In 1852, Schurz immigrated to the United States. His strong antislavery views led him to the Republican Party, and in 1860 Schurz campaigned for Abraham Lincoln (1809–1865). A year later, Lincoln, as President, appointed Schurz minister to Spain. While in Madrid, Schurz became distressed by the news of the Union defeat at the First Battle of Bull Run and the administration's lack of a firm stand on emancipation. Within six months, he returned to America, urged Lincoln to issue an emancipation proclamation, and asked for an army commission. Made a brigadier general in 1862, Schurz was later relieved of his field command after several accusations of cowardice, all of which were disproved. After the war, Schurz worked for several newspapers, the last being a German-language daily in St. Louis, before being elected to the Senate by the Missouri legislature in 1868. He then became disillusioned with the excesses of Radical Republicans and the corruption in the administration of Ulysses S. Grant (1822–1885). In 1872, Schurz chaired the **Liberal Republican Party** (*see*) convention that nominated Horace Greeley (1811–1872), who unsuccessfully contested Grant's reelection. After his own defeat for reelection to the Senate in 1874, Schurz worked for Rutherford B. Hayes (1822–1893) in the 1876 national campaign.

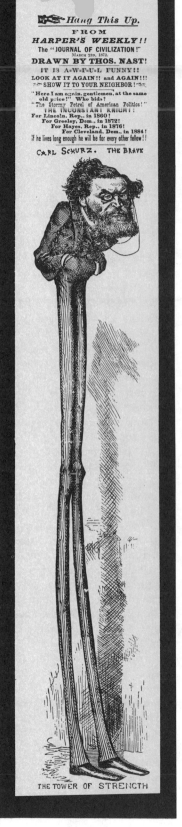

THE TOWER OF STRENGTH

Cartoonist Thomas Nast poked fun at Carl Schurz's fickle party loyalty.

After Hayes became President, he appointed Schurz his Secretary of the Interior (1877–1881). As Secretary, Schurz defended the interests of Indians, encouraged the conservation of natural resources, and introduced a merit system within the department. By 1881, Schurz was well-known as an independent reformer and expressed his views as an editor of the New York *Evening Post* and of *Harper's Weekly.* He led the revolt of the **Mugwumps** against Republican **James G. Blaine** in 1884, supporting instead Democrat **Grover Cleveland** (*see all*). From 1892 to 1900, Schurz served as president of the National Civil Service Reform League.

SCOPES TRIAL. In one of the most famous courtroom encounters in American history, the nation's leading criminal lawyer was pitted against its most eloquent orator. At issue was the constitutional interpretation of the separation of church and state. Called the Monkey Trial because it centered on the Darwinian theory of evolution, the trial—in Dayton, Tennessee—attracted nationwide attention. The defendant was John T. Scopes (1901–1970) a young biology instructor who had been discussing in his public high-school classes Darwin's theory that man is descended from the same ancestors as the ape. Fundamentalists—Christians who believe in the literal interpretation of the Bible—were outraged, and Scopes was charged with violating a state law against teaching "the theory that denies the story of the divine creation of man as taught in the Bible." Scopes, who went on trial in July, 1925, was defended by **Clarence Darrow** (*see*), who had been retained by the American Civil Liberties Union to test the constitutionality of the Tennessee statute. The state pros-

ecutor was assisted by **William Jennings Bryan** (*see*), a three-time Democratic Presidential candidate and a believer in the literal meaning of the Bible. Scopes' attorneys argued that the Tennessee law violated the constitutional principle of the separation of church and state. They further contended that evolution was consistent with the intended meaning of the Bible. The case reached a climax on the seventh day of the trial when Darrow suddenly called Bryan to testify as an expert on the Bible. In a dramatic confrontation, Darrow thoroughly bested Bryan, who was totally ignorant of science. Darrow then surprised the prosecution again by asking the jury for a verdict of guilty (in order to appeal the case to a higher court), thus keeping the frustrated Bryan from delivering a fiery closing statement that he had written. Scopes was convicted and fined $100, but the verdict was overturned by the state supreme court on a technicality. Although the constitutionality of the law was thus not settled, the trial dealt a severe blow to the Fundamentalists and served to aid the cause of Christian "Modernists," who wished to reconcile the findings of science with religion. Bryan died five days after the close of the trial. The Tennessee statute was finally repealed in 1967.

SHERMAN ANTITRUST ACT. Public protests against the increasing domination of commerce and industry by giant business combinations led Congress to pass the Sherman Antitrust Act in 1890. Named for Senator John Sherman (1823–1900) of Ohio, this law empowered the federal government to dissolve trusts and business monopolies that operated "in restraint of trade or commerce." Before 1890, several Southern and Western states had enacted laws to prevent powerful corporations from controlling prices and driving out competition within their borders, but these state statutes were ineffective in regulating businesses engaged in interstate commerce. Although several large trusts were broken up as a result of the Sherman Antitrust Act—the American Tobacco Company and the Standard Oil Company were both dissolved in 1911—the law proved largely ineffective. It failed to define such key terms as "combination" and "trust," and it did not specify what constituted "restraint of trade." These legal loopholes hamstrung the Justice Department in its attempts to prosecute monopolistic practices. In addition, Supreme Court decisions frequently supported "big business." Moreover, although the Sherman Act was intended as a curb on business abuses, it was often invoked to prosecute labor unions. Only with the strengthening of the Federal Trade Commission in the 1900s and the passage of the Clayton Antitrust Act in 1914 were giant business combines brought under more effective federal control.

SHERMAN SILVER PURCHASE ACT.
Sponsored by Senator John Sherman (1823–1900) of Ohio and enacted by Congress in 1890, this controversial legislation provided for the monthly purchase of 4,500,000 ounces of silver by the federal government. The silver bullion was to be acquired by the issuance of legal-tender Treasury notes, redeemable by the holder in either silver or gold. Seventeen years earlier, there had been no protest when the Treasury abandoned the minting of silver coins in favor of gold-backed currency. However, after large deposits of silver were discovered in the West, demands

arose from the silver-producing regions that the federal government return to a bimetal standard, thus providing a market for the Western silver. The proposal was seconded by farmers and others who wanted "inflated" currency —that is, a larger supply of cheaper money—in order to pay off their debts. The **Bland-Allison Act** (*see*) of 1878, which provided for a token purchase of silver by the Treasury, failed to satisfy the prosilver forces. The Sherman Silver Purchase Act was pushed through Congress in 1890 by lawmakers from industrial states in the East who agreed to vote with Western silver interests in return for the latter's support of the **McKinley Tariff** (*see*). Although the silver act increased the currency in circulation by $156,000,000 over a three-year period, it did not work as planned. Holders of silver certificates, especially Eastern bankers, began to cash them in for gold, drastically reducing the Treasury's gold reserves. Confidence in the American economy subsequently faltered, contributing to the **Panic of 1893** (*see*). President **Grover Cleveland** (*see*) called a special session of Congress that repealed the Sherman Silver Purchase Act in the autumn of 1893.

SIMPSON, Jerry (1842–1905).
"Sockless Jerry" Simpson was a colorful Populist member of the House of Representatives from Kansas. He had almost no formal education and worked, with varying degrees of success, as a farmer and cattle rancher in Kansas. He got his nickname in 1890, after the **People's Party** (*see*) nominated him for Congress. In a campaign speech, Simpson reputedly said that, in contrast to his opponent, a wealthy banker who wore silk socks, he, Simpson, wore none. He was immediately

tagged Sockless Jerry, a name that stuck with him the rest of his life. Simpson served three terms in the House (1891–1895 and 1897–1899). Although he seldom gave speeches, he won the respect of his opponents with his shrewd questions and witticisms.

STATUE OF LIBERTY.
Ever since she was placed on Bedloe's Island (now Liberty Island) in New York Harbor in 1886, this colossal copper statue, formally named "Liberty Enlightening the World," has served as a symbol of welcome and hope to hundreds of thousands of immigrants. Intended as a gift from France in honor of America's first century of independence, the statue was commissioned in Paris in 1875 and cost $250,000, which was raised by public donations. Liberty was designed and executed by the sculptor Frederic Auguste Bartholdi (1834–1904), who allegedly modeled her body after his mistress' and shaped her face after his mother's. The completed figure, which was 151 feet five inches tall, was shipped to America in parts in 1885. She was fitted together on a pedestal that cost $350,000, a sum also raised by donations. On the pedestal was engraved part of a sonnet by the American poet **Emma Lazarus** (*see*). On October 28, 1886, President **Grover Cleveland** (*see*) unveiled Liberty at a ceremony on Bedloe's Island. One of the largest statues in the world, Liberty bears a book of laws in her left hand, and holds a torch, which was first illuminated by bulbs in 1916, in her right. She weighs 225 tons, and her dimensions include a 35-foot waist, a 42-foot right arm, a 10-foot-thick head, and a four-foot six-inch nose. Because of weathering, the copper has turned green. A popular tourist attraction, the statue has an observation deck

Looming over a Paris street, Liberty nears completion in Bartholdi's courtyard.

George Westinghouse (*see both*), Tesla made important contributions to the field of electricity. Born in the part of Austria-Hungary that is now Yugoslavia, Tesla invented his first electrical device—a telephone mechanism—in 1881. Three years later, he immigrated to the United States. Tesla worked for a while with Edison but quit when they quarreled over the rights to an invention. Going into business for himself, Tesla experimented with transporting electricity through the use of an alternating current and thus discovered the most practical means of conducting electricity over great distances. As a result, he became involved in a controversy with Edison, who was a proponent of direct current. Westinghouse rallied to Tesla's side in the dispute and manufactured Tesla's equipment. In 1893, Westinghouse was awarded a contract to develop the power of Niagara Falls on alternating current. Tesla designed the system. From 1897 to 1905, he worked on transmitting electrical power without wires and paved the way for the development of the radio. Although the 1912 Nobel Prize in physics was originally offered to Tesla and Edison jointly, Tesla refused the honor because he still regarded Edison as an enemy. As a result, both men's names were withdrawn by the award committee.

V

VANDERBILT, Cornelius (1794–1877). Known as Commodore Vanderbilt because he made his first millions in the steamboat and shipping business, Cornelius Vanderbilt became one of America's greatest railroad magnates after the outbreak of the Civil War (*see p. 862*). Vanderbilt began his career as a ferryman be-

that holds approximately 40 people at any one time.

STEPHENS, Uriah Smith (1821–1882). Stephens helped to found the **Knights of Labor** (*see*), a union that was the most powerful labor organization in the nation in the late 1880s. Stephens had originally intended to become a Baptist minister, but when his family could not afford to pay for his studies, he went to work for a tailor. He read widely in economics and later traveled throughout Central America and the Caribbean before living for a time in California. In 1862, he helped to organize the Garment Cutters' Association in Philadelphia. Pressure from employers forced the dissolution of the union in 1869. Following this, Stephens helped organize the Holy and Noble Order of Knights of Labor, a secret national trade union. He stressed

the secret side of the group in order to protect workers from vindictive employers. As Grand Master Workman, Stephens viewed the union as the nucleus for creating cooperative ownership of all means of production. However, the union grew slowly under Stephens' leadership, and a bitter dispute over the secrecy rules arose between him and Terence V. Powderly (1849–1924). The dispute led to Stephens' resignation in 1879, and two years later the secrecy rule was abandoned. The Knights of Labor, however, continued to honor Stephens as a pioneer labor leader and, upon his death, granted $10,000 to his family.

T

TESLA, Nikola (1856–1943). Along with **Thomas Edison** and

RAPHO-GUILLUMETTE; PHOTO SIROT

E368

tween New York City and his native Staten Island and eventually got control of most of the steamboat lines in the vicinity. In 1851, at the height of the California gold rush, he opened a passenger-and-freight-carrying service between New York and California. The service was a tremendous success because it included land transit through Nicaragua, Central America, that was two days shorter and cheaper than the old Spanish land route through Panama.

Cornelius Vanderbilt

ama. Vanderbilt entered the railroad field in 1862 when he bought control of the New York & Harlem Railroad. He soon gained control of the Hudson River Railroad, and in 1867 he acquired the New York Central Railroad. In 1868, he failed in his famous attempt to gain control of the Erie Railroad, which operated between New York and Chicago. However, five years later, at the insistence of his son, **William H. Vanderbilt** (*see*), he finally extended the Vanderbilt railroad system to connect New York and Chicago by obtaining control of the Lake Shore & Michigan Southern Railway. Two years later, the Commodore completed his role as the creator of

one of America's most extensive transportation networks by buying the Michigan Central and Canada Southern Railroads.

VANDERBILT, William Henry (1821–1885). The son of **Cornelius Vanderbilt** (*see*), William H. Vanderbilt took over control of his family's great railroad empire shortly before his father's death in 1877. During the remaining nine years of his own life, he managed to increase the Vanderbilt family fortune considerably (*see pp. 862–863*). Born in New Jersey, William did not win his father's favor until he had made a success out of farming and railroad ventures on Staten Island during the Civil War. In 1864, he became his father's chief associate, and after Cornelius' death he became president of the vast network of corporations affiliated with the New York Central Railroad. William was an able railroad executive. When, despite a cut in their wages, the employees of the New York Central remained loyal to the Vanderbilts and refused to take part in the great railway strike of 1877, he rewarded them by dividing $100,000 among them. However, he incensed many people two years later when, in defending his decision to stop an unprofitable mail service between Chicago and New York, he declared, "The public be damned. I'm working for my stockholders." Because of failing health, Vanderbilt resigned his various railroad presidencies in May, 1883.

W

WEAVER, James Baird (1833–1912). A leading critic of big business interests and an advocate of "easy money," Weaver ran twice for the Presidency on third-party tickets. Raised in frontier Iowa,

Weaver practiced law prior to entering the Union Army at the start of the Civil War in 1861. As a result of his gallantry in action, he was brevetted a brigadier general in 1865. After the war, Weaver entered Iowa politics as a Republican, but his denunciations of corporate practices and his advocacy of printing vast amounts of inflated paper money soon alienated him from the party. His beliefs, however, coincided with those of the newly organized **Greenback Party** (*see*), and in 1878 he was elected to the House of Representatives as a Greenbacker. The party nominated him for President in 1880, but Weaver only polled about 300,000 votes, or slightly more than 3% of the total, and received no electoral votes. He was defeated for reelection to the House in 1882 but won again in 1884 and 1886. When Greenback strength on the national level began to decline, Weaver helped to organize the **People's Party** (*see*), which nominated him for President in 1892. This time, Weaver polled more than 1,000,000 votes, or almost 9% of the total, and received 22 electoral votes.

WESTINGHOUSE, George (1846–1914). Best known for devising the railroad air brake and electric transformers, Westinghouse held more than 400 patents for inventions in a variety of fields. While still a teen-ager in upstate New York, he designed a rotary steam engine. Westinghouse left college after three months to work in his father's agricultural tool shop. Horrified by the number of head-on train collisions caused by the inability of engineers to stop their trains quickly, Westinghouse went to work on a new braking system. He first tried to devise a brake operated by steam, but failing in this he turned to experimenting with compressed air. He secured his air-brake patent in 1869 and that same year founded the Westinghouse Air Brake Company. In time, his air brake became standard equipment on all railroads and made high-speed railroad travel safe. In 1882, Westinghouse organized the Union Switch and Signal Company to manufacture the automatic signaling devices he had also developed for railroads. Three years later, he worked out a means of conveying natural gas through pipes over long distances. Westinghouse then became interested in the transmission of electricity. Although the idea was condemned by **Thomas Edison** (*see*) as unsafe, Westinghouse, with the help of **Nikola Tesla** (*see*), constructed transformers that allowed the transmission of electricity as alternating, rather than direct, current. This made possible the transmission of electricity over long distances. In 1886, he incorporated the Westinghouse Electric Company to manufacture the transformers. By the turn of the century, Westinghouse enterprises were worth $120,000,000, and about 50,000 workers were employed in his plants. However, during the Panic of 1907, Westinghouse lost control of his companies, and in 1911 he severed his connections with them.

WILSON–GORMAN TARIFF. The Wilson-Gorman Tariff was intended to lower the high duties imposed by the **McKinley Tariff** (*see*) of 1890. However, the Senate amended the original House bill so drastically—634 changes were made—that the act had little effect. The tariff, enacted in August, 1894, was named for Representative William L. Wilson (1843–1900) of West Virginia and Senator Arthur P. Gorman (1839–1908) of Maryland. Duties were reduced from an average of 48.4% to an average of 39.9%. However, they were retained on iron and coal and newly imposed on raw and refined sugar. The new duties on sugar caused a depression in Cuba that led to the revolt that eventually precipitated the Spanish-American War in 1898. Under the tariff, wool, lumber, and copper could be imported without paying duties. The act also provided for a 2% tax on incomes over $4,000. The tax, however, was declared unconstitutional by the Supreme Court the following year. President **Grover Cleveland** (*see*), whose party was pledged to tariff reform, found the bill so weakened that he denounced it as "party perfidy and dishonor." However, he did not veto it. Under the Constitution, the bill automatically became law without his signature because the House was still in session.

WOODRUFF, Theodore Tuttle (1811–1892). T. T. Woodruff was one of the pioneers in the development of the railroad sleeping car. A native of New York City, Woodruff was apprenticed to a wagon maker when he was 16. He later began building railroad cars and was employed by the Terre Haute and Alton Railroad in Illinois to construct their coaches. In 1857, Woodruff designed and built a sleeping car. The following year, he approached Andrew Carnegie (1835–1919) with a model of his car. Carnegie, then a minor official of the Pennsylvania Railroad, brought it to the attention of the line's management. With the railroad's guarantee to purchase his sleeping cars, Woodruff began manufacturing operations in Philadelphia in 1858 under the firm name of the Woodruff Palace Car Company. However, he sold out his interests about 1862 in order to move to Ohio to enter the banking business. Carnegie later arranged the merger of the company with Woodruff's old competitor, **George Pullman** (*see*). After eight years, Woodruff returned to Pennsylvania, where he established a foundry and resumed work on his inventions. In 1872, he patented a machine for manufacturing indigo dye and another for hulling coffee beans. The expense of developing these machines, however, left him bankrupt. He was killed in 1892 when he was hit by an express train in Gloucester, New Jersey.

Y

YOUNGER, (Thomas) Coleman (1844–1916). A bank and train robber who terrorized the Midwest with **Jesse James** (*see*) in the 1860s and 1870s, Younger was born in Missouri. He served with the Confederate raider William Quantrill (1837–1865) during the Civil War and took part in the massacre of 182 persons at Lawrence, Kansas, in 1863. Younger later became a captain in the "Iron Brigade" of General Joseph O. Shelby (1830–1897). After the war, he and his brothers, Robert and James, formed an outlaw gang with Jesse James and his brother, Frank James (1843–1915). Led by Jesse, the brigands robbed banks, trains, and stagecoaches for more than 15 years. Younger is said to have been present at all the robberies and holdups the gang committed during its first 10 years. In 1876, Younger and his two brothers were wounded and captured in an attempted bank robbery at Northfield, Minnesota. All three were convicted and given life terms. Younger was released 27 years later. He then appeared in a Wild West show with Frank James, lectured occasionally, and otherwise led a law-abiding life.